Dedicated to:

Rick Giles, Rebecca Miller, John Brooks, Becky Smith, Robert Kramer, Dawn Westberry, Bruce Whittmore, Bruce Hasson, Cher Rutherford, Bruno Collins, Luanne Pulliam, Stephen Knight, Rae Josephs, Jack Davey, Sharon Savoy, Didio Barrera, and Michael Martin – *our Dance Instructors and Coaches who believed in our abilities, even when we did not, and had the wisdom and courage to push us beyond what we ever imagined – who brought us the gift of dance, created amazing choreography, and shared their excitement for ballroom dancing. Thank you for addicting us to this amazing sport!*

From Ballroom to Bottom Line...

...in business and in life

Bil Holton, Ph.D.
Cher Holton, Ph.D.
Co-authors of A Manager's Short Course to a Long Career

Liberty Publishing Group
Raleigh • Frederick • Egg Harbor

Copyright ©2001 by Bil and Cher Holton. All rights, including electronic and digital, reserved. Printed in the United States of America. No part of this book may be used, reprinted or recopied in any manner whatsoever without written permission of the authors. For information, contact www.holton-consulting.com. or Liberty Publishing Group, 4704 Little Falls Dr., Raleigh, NC 27609.

Liberty Publishing Group, Raleigh, Frederick, Egg Harbor

First Edition

Library of Congress Cataloging-in-Publication Data.
Holton, Bil. 1947–   Holton, Cher. 1950–
FROM BALLROOM TO BOTTOM LINE ... in business and in life / by Bil Holton and Cher Holton
   p. cm.

ISBN 1-893095-05-3

1 Team Development. 2 Title. 3 Personal Growth. 4 Professional Growth.

Printed and bound by CSS Publishing Company–Books on Demand, Lima, Ohio

Table Of Contents

Acknowledgements	viii
Introduction	ix
How to Use This Book	xi
A Ballroom Briefing	xiii
Adagio	20
Adding Insult to Injury	22
Asymmetry	24
Attitude	26
Dance Wisdom	28
Raising the Barre	30
Body Ceramics	32
Quote from the Pros	34
Dance Wisdom	35
Championship Moxie	36
Chassé	38
CBM	40
Cha-Cha	42
Quote from the Pros	44
Dance Wisdom	45
Circumduction	46
Complete It	48
Corté	50
Cuban Motion	52
Quote from the Pros	54
Dance Wisdom	55
Dancer's Ears	56
Ego Static	58
Emotional Glue	60
Focus	62
Gotta Dance	64

Quote from the Pros..	66
Dance Wisdom..	67
Harmonic Convergence...	68
Health Insurance...	70
Impression Concessions..	72
Improvisation..	74
Grand Jeté...	76
Junk Rehearsal..	78
Quote from the Pros..	80
Dance Wisdom..	81
Kudo Kudzu..	82
Quote from the Pros..	84
Dance Wisdom..	85
Leading...	86
Leotards and Pirouettes...	88
Line of Dance...	90
Metered Time...	92
Quote from the Pros..	94
Dance Wisdom..	95
Master of Mime..	96
Mambo Moomba..	98
Mojo..	100
Negative Space...	102
Quote from the Pros..	104
Dance Wisdom..	105
Parquet Piety..	106
The Paso Doble...	108
Pivots..	110
Promenade..	112
Quote from the Pros..	114
Dance Wisdom..	115
Quick Stepping...	116
Sweat Suite...	118
Relevé...	120
Quote from the Pros..	122

Dance Wisdom	123
Let's Rumba	124
Salsa	126
Sell the Sizzle	128
Sitstilla	130
Quote from the Pros	132
Dance Wisdom	133
The Social Contract	134
Spaceshifting	136
Staccato	138
Sync or Sink	140
Quote from the Pros	142
Dance Wisdom	143
The Syntax of Performance	144
Twinkle	146
Verbal Splinters	148
Volta	150
Waltz	152
Quote from the Pros	154
Dance Wisdom	155
About the Authors	156
More Books by the Holtons	157
How to Contact the Holtons	157

Acknowledgements

For her tireless office support, editing and moxie, we thank Nancy Eubanks, who did her part to keep this project fun and on time. She helped us raise the editing barre, kept our dancer's ears tuned, and engineered the harmonic convergence of two authors who each had his and her favorite input. She also made sure we never ran out of cocoa!

We especially want to thank all of the ballroom and DanceSport Champions, coaches, choreographers, judges and studio owners who so graciously sent us their wisdom and advice as we labored to present the best possible content. Awesome appreciation goes to all the professional dancers who have been an inspiration to us with their impressive talent, incredible stamina, unquenchable joy of dancing, and intense commitment to the professionalism of the sport.

Thanks to Donna Bowers, for her extraordinary photography. It was a challenge, but she made it happen! David Runk, with CSS Publishing B.O.D. provided the periodic nudges that kept us focused on our printing goal. We are grateful for his patience and technical advice.

As co-authors, we're giving ourselves the high-five for a most enjoyable partnership in creating this manuscript – and for applying the dance wisdom we learned along the way to complete this wonderful project. Hallelujah! It is finally a reality! Let's Rumba!

INTRODUCTION

The scene is set in Miami, Florida, the beautiful Fontainbleau Hotel. The attraction that has a standing-room-only audience filled with excitement – the United States DanceSport Championships. Ballroom dancing at its best.

Electricity fills the air as the audience sends their adulation to the performers who take their positions on the dance floor. Spectators shout the names of their favorite couples. The competitors prance and strut to the sounds of the cha-cha, rumba and swing, sending the audience into perpetual cheers, applause and fanatical outbursts of praise.

As the music prepares the dancers for the last crescendo, the audience collectively shifts forward slightly in their seats, waiting for the final majestic poses of the competitors. The energy in the ballroom is at a fever pitch as the final dance ends and the finale's theatrics force the spectators to their feet in thunderous applause.

§ § § § § § § § § §

Ballroom dancing is taking the country by storm, as indicated not only by its inclusion as an Olympic event, but by the waiting lists on college campuses to take the Ballroom Dancing course, by the movies pouring out of Hollywood, and the use of famous ballroom dances in current advertisements on television. Ballroom studios are busier than ever, and the competitions sponsored by the dance world are larger and more heavily attended than at any other time in history.

We know, because we have become addicted ourselves. We'll let Cher tell the story from her perspective.

> *We have always practiced the art of stretching our limits, pushing the envelope – whatever metaphor you want to use. In fact, we even instituted what we call "Indiana Jones" vacations – at least once a month we do something we've never done before. Bil typically selects these 'vacations'. We went white-water rafting , fire walking, and sky diving. Finally I said, "Wait a minute! It's my turn to pick. Let's do ballroom dancing!"*
>
> *Bil wasn't too thrilled about it, but good sport that he is, he participated with gusto. After our three introductory lessons, we were both hooked! We have since become totally addicted, and participate in competitions, showcases, and have even added continued ballroom dancing exhibitions to our consulting business, where we tie in the principles of ballroom dancing to team work. And that is what led us to write this book.*

As you can see, we are believers! Through our lessons, coaching sessions and practices, we have learned that in and of itself, ballroom dancing is a powerful sport, requiring incredible stamina, athleticism, skill, poise and teamwork. It is unlike any other form of dance because the performers never dance solo. Ballroom, and its competitive side, DanceSport, are partnership dances. They are relationship dance activities that require a communication between the two partners that is unequaled in any other sport. This is why we have chosen ballroom dancing as an apt metaphor for team development . . . in business and in life.

Ballroom dancing at the competitive level is a meticulous sport. It requires an extraordinary partnership between the gentleman and his partner. The couple's synergy must be exquisite, the communication must be absolutely clear and concise, their problem-solving ability has to be decisive, and their composure unruffled in the heat of competition.

Partnerships in the "real world" have many similarities to the partnerships in the ballroom dance world. It doesn't matter whether you are talking about a business team, a volunteer group, a contractor relationship, a circle of close friends, a special-projects team, a romantic couple, a sports team or a family. The same skills that make a ballroom dance couple successful apply to these partnerships as well.

From Ballroom to Bottom Line is the first partnership development book of its kind and the strategies it provides can improve the bottom line "choreography" of any team. Many of the strategies used by professional dance champions will also help individuals improve their own personal dance through life.

HOW TO USE THIS BOOK

This book is written with the knowledge that you are busy! Few of us these days have the luxury of time or energy to be able to read everything we need to read, let alone all the things we want to read. It is important to be able to grab the information we need on the run — and this book is designed to help you do just that. We've made it easy for you. *From Ballroom to Bottom Line* is designed as an "easy read." You can start anywhere, go anywhere, stop any time.

The blueprint is created for ease in personal and team development. Each minichapter focuses on an aspect of ballroom dancing. It may be a type of dance, a style or dance figure, an attitude, or an emotion, or a physical attribute related to the dance partnership. We begin by describing the concept as it relates to the world of ballroom dancing; this is followed by an application of the idea as it relates to partnerships in business and in life. Each section concludes with a "Tip From Your Coaches", featuring our tips on how you can add each concept to your repertoire and improve your dance through life.

Throughout the book, you will also discover pages we have labeled "Dance Wisdom". Contained on these pages are quotes sent to us by Ballroom and DanceSport Champions, who were kind enough to share their wisdom with us. There are also quotes by others – pieces of wisdom that have meant a lot to us as we've traveled the road of life in dancer's shoes. We hope they bring you inspiration, guidance and support as you develop all of your partnerships.

A BALLROOM BRIEFING

Since this book centers around ballroom dancing, we felt it might be useful for you to know a little about the history surrounding the sport. Here is your "Executive Briefing" – a turbo course to bring you up to date on one of our favorite kinds of partnerships – Ballroom Dancing. Obviously we cannot include all the dances and all the history. This is enough to whet your appetite . . . and give you your first taste of what has become a true passion for us. Put on your dancing shoes, and waltz through this unique book.

The Waltz

The term ballroom dancing was originally applied to dances commonly performed in eighteenth century ballrooms. Ballroom dancing, as we know it, started with the introduction of the waltz (from the old German word walzen meaning to turn or glide). Born in the suburbs of Vienna and in the alpine region of Austria, the Waltz was played in the lavish ballrooms of the Hapsburg Courts. By the end of the eighteenth century, the Austrian peasant dance (the waltz) was accepted by high society and three-quarter time rhythm was here to stay.

Interestingly, the waltz was subject to violent criticism by religious leaders of the time, who felt it was vulgar and sinful. Dance masters also opposed it, for more commercial reasons: the steps were much easier to learn than the more intricate court dances of the day.

In spite of the opposition (or perhaps because of it), the waltz became extremely popular. Queen Victoria was herself an expert ballroom dancer, with waltz being her favorite dance.

The waltz was introduced to the United States in Boston in 1834, when dance master Lorenzo Papanti, gave an exhibition in Mrs. Otis' Beacon Hill mansion. Here it was received with some resistance; in fact, social leaders declared the waltz an indecent exhibition. However, as in Europe, the waltz was warmly embraced in the United States.

In 1830, the waltz's popularity was boosted when Franz Lanner and Johann Strauss created a very fast version – and the Viennese Waltz was born.

The Tango

The ballroom version of the tango originated among the lower classes in Buenos Aires, Argentina in the early to mid 1860's. The dance was called the baile con corté (the dance with a stop). In 1910, it was performed in Paris, where it caught on quickly. It migrated to England, then to America – by Belgian-born Maurice Mouvet in New York at Louis Martin's Restaurant. The tango is characterized by a staccato movement of the head in contrast to the torso, and visually illustrates an emotional tension between the man and woman. It has been included in many Hollywood films, which has enhanced its popularity and acceptance.

The Foxtrot

The first published reference to Foxtrot was an advertisement in the July 26, 1913 issue of the New York Times. The Foxtrot was originated in the summer of 1913 by vaudevillian Harry Fox in his theatre piece Jardin de Danse. People referred to his style of dance as Fox's Trot, and the name stuck. The Foxtrot was the most significant development in all the early years of ballroom dancing, because of its combination of quick and slow steps, which permitted more flexibility and enjoyment than its monotonous one-step and two-step cousins. There was more variety in Fox's Trot than in any other dance, making it conducive for entertainment purposes. The foxtrot is often synonymous with "Fred and Ginger" – who made the dance popular in their movie musicals by dancing across the screen with seeming ease, poise and unadulterated joy.

The Rumba

The first serious attempt to introduce rumba to the United States was by Lew Quinn and Joan Sawyer in 1913. Its chief rhythmical characteristic is the "Cuban motion," which involves small steps and subtle tilting of the hips by alternately bending and straightening alternate knees. It is a sensuous dance and the exaggerated pelvic movements of the dancers added quite a different flavor to the ballroom fever which swept across the world's stages. Rumba became part of the competitive ballroom world in the late 1920's.

The Cha-Cha

The cha-cha was created in 1952 by Pierre Lavelle, after a visit to Cuba. While observing the locals performing rumba, he noticed that occasionally it was danced with extra beats. Using this idea, Lavelle returned to Britain and began teaching the concept as a new and distinct dance. The term "cha-cha" most probably derives from the Cuban dance Guaracha. Others believe it evolved onomatopoeically, from the sound of the feet during the quick "4-and-1" count (cha-cha-cha). Today, the cha-cha remains one of the most popular Latin dances on the ballroom circuit.

The Swing

Dating back to the 1920's, the swing continues to be a popular dance, filled with variations and diversity in style.

Supposedly, in 1926, a newspaper reporter was at the famous Savoy Ballroom in New York, watching the couples performing to the jazz music. He asked a local dance enthusiast named "Shorty George" Snowden what dance they were doing. Snowden had just read an article about Lindbergh's flight to Paris, the title of which was "Lindy Hops the Atlantic." The idea stuck in his head, and he said "Lindy Hop". The name stuck.

Commercial dance studios did not formally begin teaching the Lindy Hop, Swing or Jitterbug until the 1940's, when their popularity could no longer be denied. Today ballroom dancers perform East Coast Swing, West Coast Swing, Lindy, Jitterbug and Jive.

Ballroom Popularity

Vernon and Irene Castle popularized exhibition ballroom dancing and were the "darlings of ballroom" throughout the world. Sadly, in 1916 Vernon chose aviation over dancing and enlisted in the Royal Flying Corps during WWI. Much to Irene's delight, he survived his wartime; however, he was killed in 1918 in an airplane crash in Texas where he had been sent to train American pilots. Irene eventually remarried, but abandoned the stage and devoted the rest of her life to animal rights.

Their story is immortalized in The Story of Irene and Vernon Castle, starring none other than Fred Astaire and Ginger Rogers, whose magnificent footwork gave ballroom dancing a major boost in the 1930's. Fred was a well-known child vaudevillian star by the time he was seven years old. His sister, Adele, danced with Fred for over twenty years before she retired and married Lord Charles Cavendish, one of the wealthiest men in England. A year later, Fred married Phyllis Potter and signed a lucrative contract with RKO to make Hollywood movies. Although Fred danced with many beautiful and talented women, he is best remembered for his partnership with the exquisitely-talented dancer, Ginger Rogers.

Although interest in ballroom dancing slipped in the sixties, by the early seventies it enjoyed a revival, particularly on college campuses. The sixties had produced an unsettling era of rock music, reckless dancing and diminished civility—all symptoms of the turbulence of the times. By the time the seventies rolled around, many students were filled with doubts about the future of America, marriage and stable relationships. They needed stability, someone or something to hold on to, someone to commiserate with.

Social ballroom dancing seemed to fill an empty emotional space. It meant a return to couples, a revival of structured one-on-one relationships. The intimacy of "touch dancing" in a social context renewed students' beliefs in "civilized" public relationships. The return to ballroom dancing represented a symbolic revolt against the political and economic excesses of the sixties. Young people sought the security of close relationships instead of the paranoia of confrontational relationships. Ballroom dancing symbolized partnership, fellowship and camaraderie in the 70's—and it still does today.

In 1989, the term DanceSport was officially adopted to mark the distinction between competitive dancing and social or recreational ballroom dancing. In 1997 the International Olympic Committee gave full recognition to the International DanceSport Federation (IDSF), the world governing body of DanceSport.

Mark McCormack, who runs the world's largest sports marketing company, said, "There is no doubt that DanceSport has the potential to become one of the jewels in the crown in the sporting world."

Without a doubt, the DanceSport couple's partnership is an apt, modern-day metaphor for teamwork. Modern ballroom's basic structure is a hybrid of almost two hundred years of grace and beauty of evolved dance movement. It is the result of decades of learning how dance competitors' bodies mutually engineer synchronized qualities of lyricism, balance, control and style in the heat of competition. In ballroom, form, style, power and technical excellence are everything.

Competitive ballroom dancing (DanceSport) requires couples to perform exquisitely-choreographed moves in a controlled and balanced manner despite the fatigue, intensity and rigor of the competition. Ballroom dancing is art as well as science. As such it is treasured by lovers of beauty, technical expertise and grace round the world.

Ballroom dancing gives both the competitor and social dancer two things: an interior sense of shared physicality and an outward sense of the harmony between two bodies, minds and souls moving as one. Dancing is about the choreographed movement of line, form and structure in relation to time and space. Ballroom dancers are the team athletes of the performing arts. Everything the dancers do is in pairs. It is this partnership which defines championship dance couples, and it is this "well-bred" partnership that makes the team aspects of ballroom dancing so appealing to business and industry, as well as personal relationships.

Teams that want to waltz around, quickstep past, and rumba above the competition will be very interested in the team development techniques outlined in *Ballroom to Bottom Line*.

It is obvious that ballroom dancing is here to stay... and to flourish! Now, let's integrate the ballroom with the real world, and discover what we can learn and apply from this most glamorous and graceful of all sports.

Every day I count wasted in which there has been no dancing.
(Friedrich Nietzsche)

ADAGIO

So much of ballroom dancing is illusion! Before your eyes, the dancers perform gravity-defying moves, spinning quickly, accelerating at a breakneck speed, then stopping 'on a dime' to hold a one-footed pose and smile dazzlingly at the appreciative audience. One component of this thrilling impression is achieved through the concept of adagio... a generic term for a combination of slow and sustained movements designed to develop line and balance.

Only by mastering the art of adagio can dancers mesmerize with their speed. It may seem strange to talk about adagio and speed in the same sentence, but therein lies the secret. Movement of the dancer's body to rhythmic accompaniment must be accomplished with fluidity and control to look artful. When skillfully performed, adagio is the successful accomplishment of intricately-choreographed figures, movements and gestures generally beyond the physical talents of those congregated to watch these competitive ballroom dancers in awe.

Adagio requires considerable leg strength that only comes through arduous training and repetitive practice. The moves done in practice to strengthen muscles also become actual elements in the choreographed routines. Without the leg strength gained in practice, ballroom dancers who specialize in theatre arts could never perform turns and exaggerated moves gracefully, let alone attempt overhead lifts. Balance and control are central to a dancer's ballroom skill repertoire; without them, the performers' movements will hover between symphony and uncertainty.

> *To dance, put your hand on your heart and listen to your soul. (Eugene "Luigi" Facciuto)*

ADAGIO
In Business And In Life

Some people make success – in business or in life – look easy. We hear about the 'overnight success' or the 'perfect relationship'. Just realize that this is only an illusion. Successful people live by the Adagio principle. They know that success only comes through slow, but sustained and purposeful movement toward defined personal and/or business objectives. Clearly defined lifestyle adagio keeps you balanced and helps you prioritize important responsibilities and involvements so you can weather 21st Century realities imposed at work and at home. Strong adagio weakens the affect of disquieting outside forces. Uncompromised, purposeful movement is the key.

Whether articulated or not, daily acts of focused, purposeful movement toward the accomplishment of strategic goals is the "intricate choreography" needed to produce success in business and life. Lifestyle adagio is movement that brings momentum. As momentum builds, your confidence and positive expectations grow.

Whether you are facing challenges at home or at work, if you confuse activity with accomplishment you will always 'hover between symphony and uncertainty." Families, work teams or social groups who transfuse activity with accomplishment see very quickly that luck favors momentum.

TIP FROM YOUR COACHES TO BUILD ADAGIO: Sometimes you have to go slow to go fast. Take the time to be sure everyone you are partnering with shares the same vision of success, and understands their role in making it happen. Then take small, purposeful movement toward those goals – every day.

ADDING INSULT TO INJURY

There is no dogma in dance. Dancing strips away all physical and emotional lies. There are a significant number of choices that are crucial to a dancer's longevity and health. No matter how athletically strong or well-conditioned a dancer is, the deeper the plié or the more extended the leg crawl, the greater the vulnerability to the knees. All competitors know that the ghosts of old traumas caused by bad habits or foolishness persist long past the initial healing. Serious injury or the accumulation of a series of chronic minor injuries can result in an abbreviated or abruptly-ended dance career.

Torn, damaged muscles will never be quite the same. Healing is the body's attempt to replace damaged tissue at the site of the injury using scar tissue as one of the structural healing agents. Although scar tissue is generally stronger than the tissue it replaces, it is not as pliable or elastic. Synovial fluid lubricates bones and lymphatic fluid lubricates muscles. When these lubricants thin out as we age, the healing process takes longer—especially when all the errors of body abuse begin to surface. Since cartilage and ligaments have little blood supply and take longer to heal than muscles, any injury to these areas presents long-term problems.

There is nothing more frustrating than having the passion to perform, yet knowing the body refuses to cooperate. The accumulated abuse on tired or weakened muscles, joints, tendons, and ligaments takes its toll, adding insult to injured egos.

ADDING INSULT TO INJURY
In Business And In Life

No matter how talented, well-funded, or academically-credentialed you are, if you accept marginal performance for any reason, you are doomed to failure. Self-defeating habits are the accumulated sediment of lethargy, disinterest and distrust that affect you wherever you are.

Chronic mediocrity is partnership scar tissue at its absolute worst, and it destroys productive relationships. In business, disempowered or incompetent leadership perpetuates this kind of team lethargy, adding insult to injury.

People and organizations plagued with these performance maladies unwittingly depend on the dogmas of encrusted policies and procedures to bandage relationship wounds. However, the medicine both teams and families need is "synovial salve," that is, communication infused with sensitivity, compassion, decisiveness and energy.

Some lifestyle injuries are easily cured by administering reminders of important commitments; reasserting established agreements, verifying key responsibilities, assessing progress, etc. Other, more serious lifestyle injuries like emotional "embezzlement," moral bankruptcy or physical insubordination must be removed to improve the chances of recovery, because the only dogma in lifestyle injury is the lack of faith in each other.

TIP FROM YOUR COACHES: Pay attention to small warning signs of relationship injuries, and deal with them before they become traumatic. Have occasional symbolic recommitments to infuse energy and excitement into important relationships.

ASYMMETRY

When dancers engage in repetitive motions like kneeling constantly on the same knee or jumping then landing on the same foot, some profound change is inevitable in the affected area. Every set of muscles has its antagonist. When one muscle becomes stronger or is more developed than a corresponding muscle, the resultant asymmetry threatens the dancer's physical stability and flexibility. If the repetitive pressure placed on certain load-bearing joints becomes habitual, it will threaten a performer's amateur or professional dance career.

Much of the excitement of dance, particularly with the sharpness of the rhythms, is created by asymmetric figures. However, all asymmetrical movements cause physical fall-out. When a choreography requires a dancer to perform a repetitive but asymmetrical move (for example, a spin on the right knee), they will build into their practice a similar move with the opposite body part (in this example, the left knee). They do this to ensure an equal strengthening of both sides, thereby avoiding asymmetry in their body development and skill.

Being overly conservative is unacceptable, whether it applies to unused muscles or unused talent. At the same time, over-use of healthy body parts causes asymmetry. This realization prompts good dancers to add anatomy, kinesiology, physiology and nutrition to their dance syllabus.

> *When Fred Astaire was asked how he came up with all his unique routines, such as using furniture, golf clubs, etc., he replied: "I don't know...you don't know if these things will work until you try them."*

ASYMMETRY
In Business And In Life

Lifestyle asymmetry occurs when non-productive assumptions about people, tradition, values and technologies go unchallenged. Wedged tightly between 1000-bubble pert charts at work and walls of indifference at home, people suffering from asymmetrical lifestyle habits are constantly stressed and demoralized. Attempts to rebound by using the 'same old, same old' kinds of stuff reinforce a debilitating lifestyle, sending people and organizations in vicious, unproductive, predictable circles.

We do this whenever we adopt worn-out strategies, defend the status quo, overuse the same problem-solving techniques, and settle for mediocrity. Over-use of any habit, talent, behavior or procedure creates obsolescence. Needless redundancy shackles accomplishment and causes people and organizations to spin on "sorry-go-rounds" of unproductive activity.

Symmetry can be re-established by seeking a balance between tradition and innovation, encrusted beliefs and spontaneous possibilities, old assumptions and new ideas. People living symmetrical lifestyles value diversity, resiliency and planned change and discard asymmetrical habits. Those who enjoy symmetrical lifestyles know that "being overly conservative is not acceptable, whether it applies to unused muscles or unused talent."

TIP FROM YOUR COACHES: Be aware of your strengths, but also recognize weaknesses and work to transform and strengthen them. Force yourself and those with whom you are partnering to "exercise" weak areas, in order to become strong and symmetrical in your dance with life.

ATTITUDE

In serious DanceSport competition, attitude is the key to "sell" the dance. It is all a game, of course, but a game practiced by those who know attitude is everything. Attitude, as it applies to ballroom competition etiquette, is rhythmical play. In the strictest sense, however, it is not an act, because the dancers are not acting. There's a saying in ballroom circles that the best dancers do not do the attitude, they express the attitude which the lyrics and rhythm of a particular dance demands. Dancers may be shy or reserved off the dance floor, but during practice and competitions, dancers morph into their DanceSport personas and "sell" the essence of the dance.

Doing the attitude is not the same thing as being the attitude. Authenticity is required. Attitude is everything. Competitors who emote the lyrical soul of the dance will always score higher at dance competitions than couples who are technically excellent, but soulfully deficient. Exquisite arm and hand gestures, body alignments and delicate styling all come from the inside out. Dance coaches can help competitors engineer the "look," but any subsurface pensiveness, automatic smiles or counterfeit emotions on the part of the couple usually leak into their performance. The judges will notice and so will the audience.

> *From the beginning we had a very good chemistry. That helped us to be successful in our dancing. We weren't the best suited physically... Other couples look more beautiful and matched. But in the end, you have to... have emotion.*
> *(Pierre Allaire, 12 times Canadian Champion)*

ATTITUDE
In Business And In Life

The ultimate testimony to the pursuit of happiness is not so much what we get out of our work or our families, but what we bring to both. When organizations hire, accept or inherit new people, and when families grow, each environment hopes it will grow good attitudes. People with good, positive attitudes bring harmony and positive expectations. The atmosphere is filled with pleasantness, cooperativeness, esprit de corps and loving relationships.

Teams plagued by members with poor attitudes eventually suffer from competence anorexia. Productivity erodes because the team's energies are divided. Focusing on tasks is difficult when members have to maneuver time and resources around bad attitudes. "Selling" teamwork is impossible when the team has to tip toe around productivity grinches and relationship trolls. Negative family "atmospherics" cause grumpiness, too.

As in the dance world, you can have all the right words, wear the right "image" clothes, and engineer the right "look" – but in the end, it's your attitude that sells you. People can spot a fake a mile away.

Hire the right attitudes at the office when you can, and fire the wrong attitudes if you must. In families it's a bit tougher, because we're held together by DNA instead of organizational charts. But we can still require civility. Although positive attitudes, like morality, cannot be legislated, they can be rewarded. Selling a wholesome attitude is an inside-out job that is contagious if it's real.

TIP FROM YOUR COACHES: You are in complete control of your attitude. Make a conscious choice to be positive and enthusiastic. Don't walk away from bad attitudes – RUN!

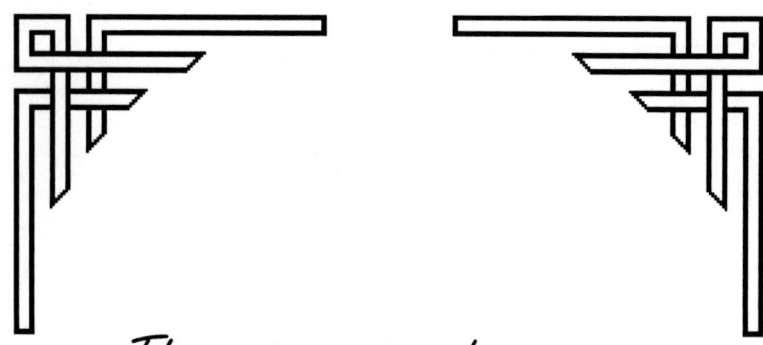

The most important dance step in your routine is the one that you are doing. Too many people go through their dance routines worrying about what is coming up next or what they just messed up, rather than perfecting the step they are doing. Running a business is the same way. (People) must focus on the job at hand.

(Gary and Diana McDonald, 9 times United States 10 Dance Champions.)

DANCE WISDOM
(Ask yourself: How do these quotes relate to my business and my life?)

It matters not how sharp and well our bodies are, when the head's not right, the body is in danger. When the sense of self is an unresolved battlefield, there's work that has to be done.
(Daniel Nagrin, <u>How to Dance Forever</u>)

I dance every day and train with weights every other day. I eat clean: no salt, no sugar. I eat light: six small meals a day instead of three large ones, and I drink 100 ounces of water every day. (Gregory Hines, legendary tap dancer)

I'll dance for them in the woods. I'll dance at the side of a lake. If there's a clearing or a good space, and I'm not too tired, I'll dance. (Jacques d'Amboise, retired principal, Dancer of the New York City Ballet and Organizer of the Trail Dance, an exploit that took him and thousands of others the entire length of the 2160-mile Appalachian Trail.)

Some people seem to feel that good dancers are born. All the good dancers I've known have been taught or trained.
(Fred Astaire, legendary dancer and entertainer)

RAISING THE BARRE

Barre work, or Beinschwingen (the waist-high hand-rail used in ballet dance studios) is essential for ballroom dancers who want to add theatre arts to their repertoire. However, all DanceSport competitors could use a little time at the barre. Besides limbering and stretching every cubic inch of a dancer's body, the barre teaches competitors about the containment of the body's line and center. It is the mechanism which helps the body learn its own somatic geography from head to foot.

Whatever the movement along the barre, the body is always controlled from the center or solar plexus. Alignments of arms, legs and pelvis originate from the center of the body. Barre work is never done. Actually, it is never supposed to be "over with." Beinschwingen is a permanent conditioning accessory in a truly world class competitor's dance life. Balance, control and flexibility are the essential "deliverables" associated with the barre. Without these practice preps, a dancer's lack of physical conditioning will show on the dance floor. With them, a dancer is always "raising the barre".

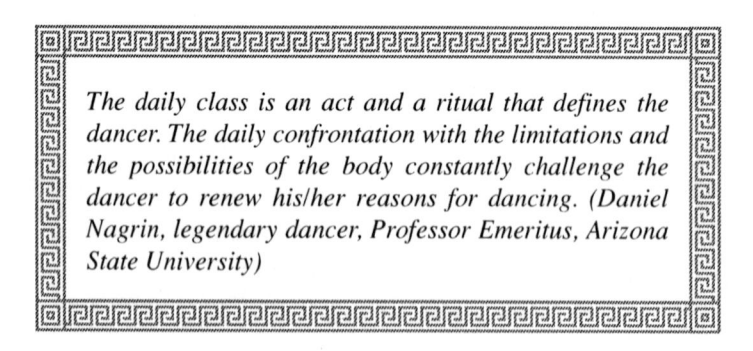

> *The daily class is an act and a ritual that defines the dancer. The daily confrontation with the limitations and the possibilities of the body constantly challenge the dancer to renew his/her reasons for dancing. (Daniel Nagrin, legendary dancer, Professor Emeritus, Arizona State University)*

RAISING THE BARRE
In Business And In Life

The only way we can truly elevate work performance and add more spice to life is to raise the barre. Raising the barre in home and work environments means providing co-workers and family alike with performance "hand-rails." These "handrails" are the social, spiritual, technical, administrative and financial supports that help guarantee defined objectives. Failure to provide lifestyle-friendly handrails turns objectives into objections because people need legitimate, not pretentious support. Objectives themselves become barriers to performance when people have nothing to hold onto to remain productive.

Rules, policies and procedures which fail to support agreed-upon goals must be modified to conform to shared expectations – or eliminated altogether. The same thing applies to lagging or obsolete technologies, unproductive political alliances, and unhealthy relationships: change them or eliminate them. Lifestyle environments, like dance environments, need the "balance, control and flexibility" of the barre to remain centered and competitive.

As people experience on-going support, they become more willing to "raise their own Barre" and outperform themselves.

TIP FROM YOUR COACHES: Keep stretching yourself, but stay focused and centered on your values and objectives (your barre to keep you aligned). As you continue to "Raise your Barre" and push the envelope of your comfort zones, you'll discover increased flexibility and balance.

BODY CERAMICS

Posture is the barometer of excellence for both the American Smooth and International Standard ballroom dances. It is the somatic political statement of confidence, virtuosity and training, and – to anyone who can read body language – a clear message from the dancer's soul.

Posture is the couple's emotional history made visible. Poor dance frame is not merely bad alignment or a momentary lapse in focus. It is often the bitter memory of less-than-gratifying dance experiences.

All dancing is from the inside out. It matters not how well dancers have mastered correct alignment and the "textbook frame." Unresolved tensions turn the "correct" look into a straightjacket look. Pent-up frustration makes a beautiful back or leg line look fragile. Self-doubt makes an elegant styling gesture look tentative or "broken."

Dancers who deny the essence of their personal worth have a difficult time concealing emotional pain on the dance floor. Their lack of confidence shows. Self-doubt manifests itself in slight frame misalignments, frame breaks and dozens of other postural miscues.

Dancers call these faulty alignments "body ceramics." The outward appearance of a dance couple, riddled with self-doubt, makes the couple appear marionette-like, more mannequin than human. When the "inner dancer" is poised and centered, every step, gesture and body movement becomes a reflection of the inner stillness that underwrites the dancer's success. The invisible soul and the material body are one, turning a ceramic look into a dynamic look of confidence and poise.

BODY CERAMICS
In Business And In Life

Remember the old adage: what you are doing speaks so loudly I cannot hear what you are saying"? We sabotage partnerships on a regular basis when we let old baggage interfere with relationships. We may say the right things, but our body will give us away every time.

Sometimes colleagues, friends, family, in-laws and "outlaws" are coated with thin veneers of respectability, suitability and professionalism. They seem to say the right things and do the right things to maintain political correctness, but there is an underlying feeling that something is not quite right. There is a hint of facade sheathed in the polished voices and mechanical smiles – an innate iciness whenever personal contact is made.

When individuals hide behind a facade of eliteness, it often shields underlying vulnerabilities, stemming from fears, performance deficiencies and fragile egos. People like this have lost the passion for work or play, but want the pay, power and companionship that go with the interpersonal territory. These people are more ceramic than real.

It is nearly impossible to project the confidence and poise necessary for an "award-winning" partnership when one or more of the partners is suffering from body ceramics. Take time to work through the baggage so you can move the relationship to a new level of success.

TIP FROM YOUR COACHES: Listen to your partners' body language. If you are getting mixed messages, or sensing an uneasiness simmering below the surface, schedule time to sit down and talk about it. Share your perceptions, then listen. Work through the hard ceramics of any facade, so you can put a new face on the relationship.

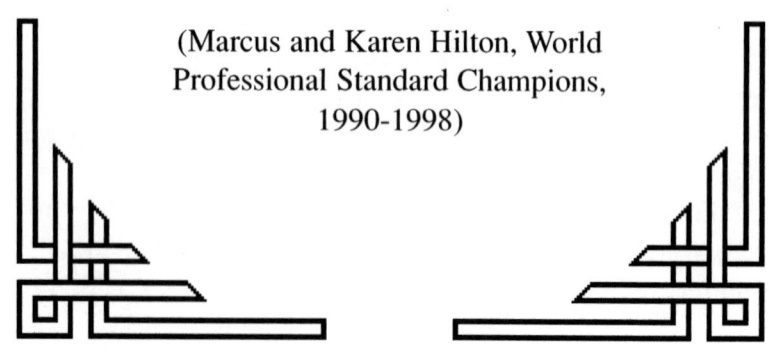

Throughout our dancing career we always thought of the "3D" effect:

DISCIPLINE, DEDICATION and DETERMINATION.

If you can concentrate on this throughout your practice and competition at the same time as enjoy and show that you enjoy your work, you will always be successful.

(Marcus and Karen Hilton, World Professional Standard Champions, 1990-1998)

DANCE WISDOM
(Ask yourself: How do these quotes relate to my business and my life?)

This is a sport that teaches you respect for the opposite sex. (That's) why it's an important social activity. If the man is too possessive or pushy or protective, the lady won't be able to do her part. In the end, it's an equal relationship.

> (Lee Wakefield, two-time national theater arts champion.)

I don't try to dance better than anyone else, only better than myself. (Mikhail Baryshnikov)

I think the reason dance has held such an ageless magic for the world is that it has been the symbol of the performance of living.

> (Martha Graham, legendary performing arts dancer and choreographer)

To catch the public, dances must have a personality and a pattern. The times my dances have clicked are the times they had a reason, when they told a part of the story, and when they belonged in the plot.
(Fred Astaire, legendary dancer and entertainer)

CHAMPIONSHIP MOXIE

The physical and mental stamina required to compete in Latin and American Rhythm dances is staggering. Couples must be in excellent condition, and that includes nurturing and maintaining a positive attitude. For example, five dances comprise the International Latin dance competition. The couple's final dance, the jive, is the most physically demanding and is purposely placed last in the set. Dancers are swung, spun, syncopated into press lines, twirled, somersaulted and sometimes rocketed in sync with lively rock-and-roll rhythms.

Placing jive last in the five dance set is a purposefully sadistic test of the couple's moxie. Even after the exhaustion of the preemptory rounds the competitors must conceal any fatigue, doubts, pain or lagging spirit during their final performance. Expectations are as high for the last dance as the first, regardless of the rigor of the marathon of heats which has brought the couples to the finals.

The trip to become one of the final six contestants is an enervating process. As many as fourteen to sixteen heats may be required, with as many as two dozen highly-talented couples in each heat. The field is narrowed to the semifinals, where twelve outstanding couples compete for the final six positions. From these elite six emerge the three medal winners and the ranked runners-up. The dancers' power, poise, and championship moxie are rewarded as the couples proudly accept their prizes and applause at the awards ceremony.

CHAMPIONSHIP MOXIE
In Business And In Life

Successful businesses and families have one common denominator – persistence. They succeed because they persevere. They persevere because they have moxie. They know that the trip from problem inception to problem solution can be an exhausting process...but they also know they must manage the fatigues, doubts, pains and lagging spirits which occur during the contest between will power and won't power.

Tenacity is one of the chief measures of anyone's overall success. Those partnerships who can sustain their energy, enthusiasm and commitment in the midst of exhaustion, frustration and roadblocks possess Championship Moxie.

The struggle is worth it! The gain in self-confidence after weathering serious difficulties is immense, and contributes to a sense of pride and togetherness.

TIP FROM YOUR COACHES: When you hit rocky roads in your relationships, do not give up. Remind each other of why you are there, and reinforce the goals you share. Remember that everyone experiences fatigue and frustration. Champions work through it and come out with rewards of increased self-confidence, improved partnerships and a shared sense of accomplishment.

CHASSÉ

Simply put, chassés are side steps in ballroom dancing. They are meant to accent forward progressions and to create novel movements which add a touch of elegance and sophistication to the choreography. Chassés are toe movements in half time and complement the classical heel-to-toe steps in all smooth dances. These side-to-side movements also occur in the rhythm Latin dances and are usually accomplished with the Cuban motion in full swing.

In addition to the aesthetics of properly timed and executed chassés, the chief functional applications of the side movements allow competitors to tactfully maneuver around other dance couples on crowded floors or to position themselves diagonally to execute the next series of movements. Whether dancers take chassés diagonally or forward, the side-to-side steps add a touch of flare to a dance couple's competitive repertoire, while getting them where they need to be.

One tap dancer defied the concept of having a specialty area. He did everything includingacrobatic turns, graceful Soft Shoes, Buck and Wings, and powerful rhythm tap dance. And if that alone were not enough, this man did it all on one leg – and a peg. Known as Peg Leg Bates, his ambition was: "to be so good that I would surpass the two-leg dancers!" And in many cases, he did! (From The Greatest Tap Dance Stars and Their Stories, 1900-1955)

CHASSÉ
In Business And In Life

Lifestyle chassés are a necessary ingredient to move us forward in business and in life. As we work together with others to achieve defined objectives, we often encounter obstacles which affect our performance. Teams suffer because of poor leadership, unclear roles, limited resources, or lack of accountability. Families encounter circumstances which challenge family unity and happiness.

Most of the time we deal with resistance head-on. But sometimes we have to side-step weighty issues in order to meet our goals. As we face the challenges associated with bottom line management, we may have to chassé around disappointments and conflict, bothersome resource shortages, exasperating personalities, unforgiving policies and regulations, and unwelcome changes in work and family environments. Confronting relatives, friends and co-workers alike can test our patience and resources.

Lifestyle chassés can keep teams competitive and families civil. Side-stepping emotional potholes often keeps us from getting knocked out of alignment. Chassés to the right and chassés to the left enable us to add a little zig to our zag as we meet and exceed work or family responsibilities. By implementing the concept of chassés into our partnership repertoire, we can get where we need to be, with style and pizzazz.

TIP FROM YOUR COACHES: When facing a seemingly insurmountable obstacle, refocus your thinking. Instead of complaining, change your question. Ask: how can we chassé around it? Chassé to handle obstacles with poise, confidence, style and flair. Remember: there is more than one way to do just about everything!

CBM
(CONTRARY BODY MOVEMENT)

Competitive ballroom dancers must understand and be able to execute contrary body movement (CBM). The level of technical difficulty is so complex that it is not taught to beginners. Contrary body movement occurs when the dancer's body turns slightly, from the hips upwards, so that the opposite hip and shoulder rotate toward the moving leg. For example, if the gentleman steps forward on his left foot, his right shoulder and hip will be turned slightly forwards. It is a common fault to break at the waist and turn only the shoulders.

A variation of CBM is called CBMP (contrary body movement position). Simply put, when the gentleman steps across his body keeping his body facing the line of dance, he will be in CBMP. Contrary body movement position is used on all outside steps (stepping outside the partner). Both CBM and CBMP add eloquence and style to otherwise standard dance progressions.

Dancers must be in good physical condition and have at least a couple of year's ballroom dancing experience before they add CBM or CBMP to their repertoire. While there are some disco moves in ballroom rhythm dances, adding CBM and CBMP too soon could lead to a slipped "disc-o" or two.

You need to be a strong individual dancer to be a strong partner—you need to stand on your own two feet...
(John and Cathi Nyemchek, U.S. 10-Dance Champions)

CBM
In Business And In Life

Turning contrary body movement into lifestyle CBM is as much an advanced technique for families and teams as it is for ballroom dancers. Lifestyle CBM requires seemingly contradictory movement towards a singular purpose. Lifestyle CBM tests our skill and patience because it generally occurs in a climate which preaches togetherness, but fosters hidden agendas and covert alliances.

Examples of environments requiring CBM include organizations that reward individual performance but expect teamwork; appoint cross-functional teams, but limit shared resources; or praise quality improvements, then downsize the team. Hostile family and social environments include those in which members work at cross-purposes, exploit a loved one's vulnerabilities, or allow bad habits and addictions to deplete a family's resources.

CBM-ing troublesome obstacles requires a high degree of trust, confidence and synergy. Overtly, work or social relations in CBM mean playing by the rules. Covertly, we must work behind the scenes with colleagues or friends who provide the necessary money, power, support and/or resources in spite of the organization's or family's ineptitude. Sometimes we need confidential outside help to solve common problems. That is the CBM side of business, family and personal relationships.

TIP FROM YOUR COACHES: When faced with a partnership riddled with contradictions, do what you have to do to function within that environment (CBM). However, look for supporters who can help you achieve your goals. Be careful who you trust, and work to change environments as quickly as you can – to ones that are in alignment with your values, beliefs and goals.

CHA-CHA

The character of the cha-cha is like the music itself. It is energetic, flamboyant, playful and engaging with the mood set for plenty of innocent fun. The name itself is a product of the splitting of the fourth beat of the music into the familiar cha-cha-cha chassé movements either forward, backward or sideways. The cha-cha adds two Cuban rhythms, the danzón and the montuno to create its stylistic impression.

The cha-cha is a rhythm dance and, as such, is a dance of play, gaiety and flirtation. It involves many turns, spins, chassés and press lines which accentuate the cavalier mood of the dance. Competitively, cha-cha lyrics and rhythms ask dancers to hit their technical marks, but to hit them while the couple is dramatizing the playfulness of party-goers. It gives competitors the opportunity to see purposeful play as a legitimate part of performance.

During the learning phase, you have to fake the fun while you are concentrating on the steps and working to create the "cuban motion" sway of the hips. Once you have the mechanics built into your muscle memory, the fun begins. That is when the cha-cha becomes a magnetic dance that attracts fun to dancers and spectators alike.

If you aren't having fun in your work, fix the problem before it becomes serious. Ask for help if you need it. If you can't fix it and won't ask for help, please go away before you spoil the fun for the rest of us. (Russ Walden)

CHA-CHA
In Business And In Life

When we incorporate fun into the rigors of our work, we are cha-cha-ing our way through assigned tasks. Many of us believe there is a time for work and a time for play. We separate the two activities as though work and play are irreconcilable opposites. Philosophically, we believe work is serious and play is frivolous. So, merry-making and money-making are considered incompatible. For the workaholic us, work itself has become a sort of morphine, deadening us to the positive effects of purposeful play during work hours.

This resistance to incorporating a reasonable amount of levity into our work keeps us plastic and soulless. Unfortunately, it is this collective tightness that causes us to miss the joy of successfully completing a task ahead of schedule or feeling a sense of pride for a job well done. Seriousness has its place, but so does a little fun. Moderate amounts of lightheartedness and exuberance soften the rough edges of life. Like competitive dance couples, we can find more satisfaction by cha-cha-ing playfully, but purposefully, toward defined objectives or around obstinate family members and friends.

TIP FROM YOUR COACHES: Add a sense of fun and play to your work. Try singing (yes–out loud!); posting cartoons and fun quotes; displaying photos of things you enjoy. Move to a cha-cha rhythm as you move from one task to another. We recommend adopting the phrase: 'Are we having fun yet?' as a team mantra.

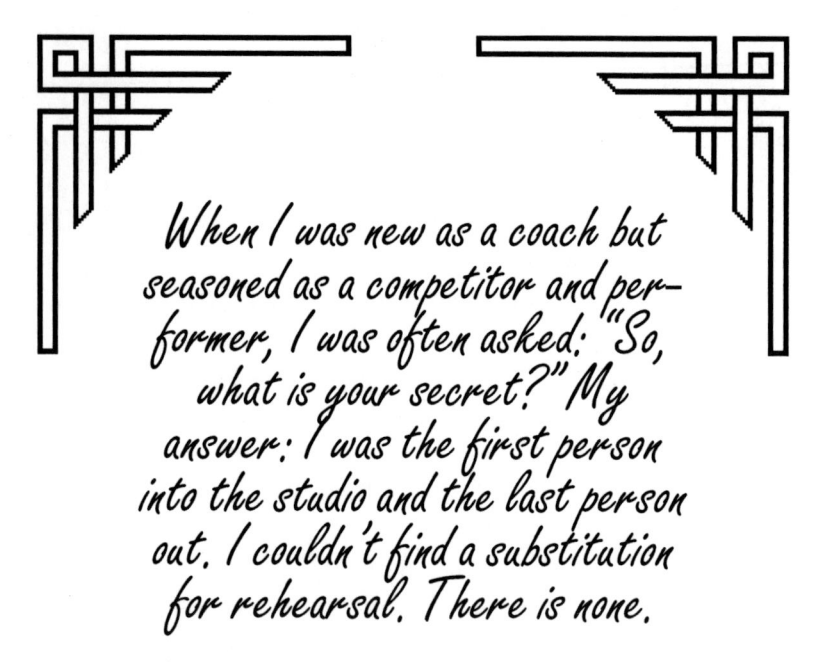

When I was new as a coach but seasoned as a competitor and performer, I was often asked: "So, what is your secret?" My answer: I was the first person into the studio and the last person out. I couldn't find a substitution for rehearsal. There is none.

(Cher Rutherford, former U.S. Champion in American Style Open Smooth and Rhythm, 1980, 1981; former US Champion Theatrical Style, 1981, 1982; Championship Adjudicator A+B+C+D+ and World Class Adjudicator; Examiner with Fred Astaire National Council of Dance; Imperial Society of Teacher of Dance; National Committee Member and Secretary, U.S.I.S.T.D. Fellow T/A Branch; U.S.I.S.T.D. Licentiate Latin and Ballroom)

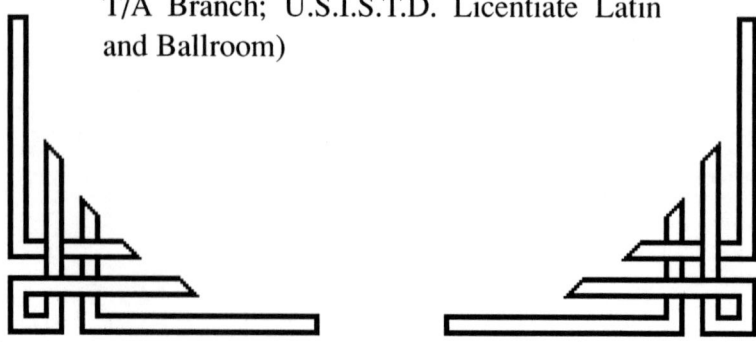

DANCE WISDOM
(Ask yourself: How do these quotes relate to my business and my life?)

Ballroom dancing is a hobby, hard work, lots of monetary expenditures, and great happiness in the long run. People who get meshuga (crazy) from it need to reevaluate their priorities and realize that to take it so seriously when you are an amateur, supposedly doing it for fun and relaxation, is harmful to you and those around you.

(Alita Clayman, dancer, writer)

I love to dance, to teach, to draw...I now realize I can draw with my body or I can sit and dance with my hand and it is one and the same.
(Candida Cutierrez, dancer, artist)

We're all dancers and we know the feeling of working with a coach who is able to help give us corrections that greatly improve our dancing. A championship title...may not...be in my control. What is in my control is my own dancing and my feelings about it.

(Victor Fung, finalist in the under 21 British Blackpool Dance Festival, 1996)

A dancer who fears work and failure should get out immediately. It is extremely hard work. If you don't take joy in it, if you're not inspired by it, it is not for you.
(Agnes de Mille)

CIRCUMDUCTION

One of the important insights for ballroom dancers is understanding that the action possible for each joint in the body determines the range of movement available for any dance movement. Different joints have different actions for different functions. Some joints, like the knee, allow only two kinds of movement. They either flex (bend) or extend (straighten). Other joints, such as the hip joint, can flex and extend. All of our appendages (arms, head, legs) can rotate at the point they are attached to the torso. Our arms rotate at the shoulder, the head on top of the spine at the neck and the leg at the hip.

Circumduction is the term dancers use to describe the action that occurs when one end of a body part is fixed (attached) so that the other end can trace a circular path in space. The head, arm, wrist, waist and ankle are all fixed body parts that enable dancers to perform choreographed circular movements.

Forcing a joint to perform a movement it wasn't designed for can cause problems. Knees sent in awkward directions or arm rotations hyper-extending the shoulder cuff, for example, can result in serious injury. Jerking someone's arms or lifting a dance partner improperly can cause rotator cuff and disk injuries. Respecting the limits and range of body parts allow dancers to take care of the instrument they use the most on the dance floor—their body.

Music unites us to dance as one. It is our vehicle. It takes us places we never thought we could go.
(Steven Mitchell, legendary lindy hopper)

CIRCUMDUCTION
In Business And In Life

Lifestyle circumduction is a business's or family's coordinated action around a solid base of values, guiding principles and work ethics. These values, principles and code of ethics are the basis of strong relationships. Everything we do revolves around this operational centrality. We face so many menacing challenges today that the sheer weight, mass and momentum of obstacles can derail us if we're not practicing lifestyle circumduction.

Teams travelling past narrow organizational policies and procedures, through fussy cross-functional kingdoms, and across finicky economic and technological drawbridges need a low center of gravity to avoid being knocked over by bureaucratic sentinels protecting the status-quo. Solid values can help families settle important differences, understand each other's view points and obey family rules.

Behavior, underwritten by superior work habits and uncompromised ethics, will always produce good results. Our character will help us chassé, spin, and pivot past any obstacle. Our collective character is the axis around which everything else revolves, moves and has its being. Forcing family or team members to do things outside the norms and values can damage relationships and erode the trust and stability so necessary to sustain worthwhile relationships.

TIP FROM YOUR COACHES: When you are asked to do something that violates your ethical or philosophical beliefs, "chasse, spin or pivot" past the unethical suggestion. Emphatically say 'no!' Within any partnership, make time to develop a set of Key Operating Procedures, which will guide your circumduction, allowing free and unencumbered range of motion to achieve your goals.

COMPLETE IT

Except for their brief mention on this page and the next, (and in the team leadership description pages) the words *follow, following,* and *followership* as they relate to the lady's role in reacting to a gentleman's lead will not appear anywhere else in this book. Competitively speaking, the term *follow* makes no sense, since leading is initiating movement or direction which has to be continued (completed) in a complimentary manner by the lady. Technically the terms *follow* and *following* are inappropriate in competitive DanceSport, because the lady is as familiar with the dance steps, patterns and choreography as the gentleman, so she doesn't have to follow him anywhere!

Once a gentleman initiates the move with a proper lead, the lady, as intelligent as she is beautiful, simply completes the intended figure or pattern as gracefully and dramatically as her experience and skills allow. The important thing to remember is that completion means equity and equity places equal responsibility on each of the dance partner's shoulders. (Or is that feet in this case?) Women only "follow" in social dance relationships where they have limited dancing experience with the gentleman. Competitive couples know where the other is going and hopefully take their partnership to the winners' podium.

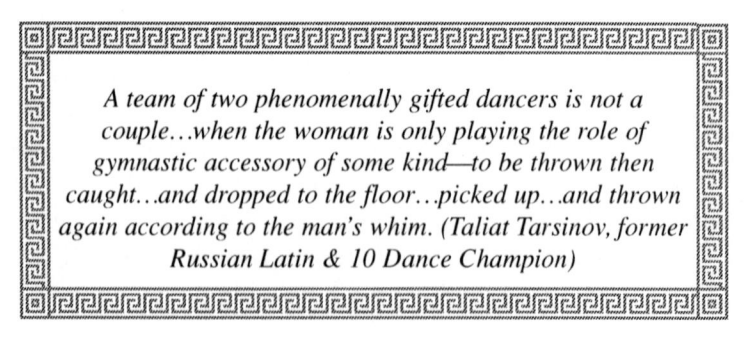

> *A team of two phenomenally gifted dancers is not a couple...when the woman is only playing the role of gymnastic accessory of some kind—to be thrown then caught...and dropped to the floor...picked up...and thrown again according to the man's whim. (Taliat Tarsinov, former Russian Latin & 10 Dance Champion)*

COMPLETE IT
In Business And In Life

Three of the most over-used and misunderstood words in business and family relationships today are follow, following and followership. Dictionary definitions for "follow" include: to go after; to obey; to carry out fully or completely. "Follower" has synonyms like: supporter, disciple, partisan, believer, and so on. "Followership" simply put, means the ability to follow a leader. Calling your attention to the dictionary meanings of these words is an appeal your common sense and gives us some wiggle room in case you think we are playing semantics.

In our defense, several dictionary definitions of the word "complete" are: bring to a conclusion, finish; end; to successfully execute or effect fruition; to make it one's business. Semantics aside, the synonyms for the word "complete" seem to describe our partnerships in business and in life better than to "follow" or "follower" or "followership."

Leadership, socially or professionally, is the ability to inspire people to achieve defined objectives. Lifestyle completion is the capacity to translate vision into practical reality. Once the vision is conceptualized and the strategic direction defined, a leader's job is to get out of the way and let talented and inspired people "successfully complete" what they have conceptually started. In today's nano-second world, seldom can we take people where neither of us has been. We must arrive together in a partnership of initiation and completion, cause and effect, strategy and tactics.

TIP FROM YOUR COACHES: You don't have to drag people where you want them to go. Determine your vision; set clear expectations; clarify the roles; provide the training to ensure everyone possesses the necessary skill; then get out of the way and let others complete it.

CORTÉ

In the Tango -- to keep the mood of dance alive, dancers use cortés to demonstrate metaphorical tension or conflict between the dance partners. The corté is a sudden halt in the dance progression while the couple resolves their conflict. Such a halt, though not a figure in itself, adds a sense of heightened suspense to the "tangoed" web the couple weaves. In reality the gentleman must indicate and then clarify his intentions to the lady – or vice versa.

There are many elaborate styling devices used to "fill" cortés so the couple can resolve pretended differences. One method is the Shoeshine technique, which is accomplished with the gentleman on his left foot and knee slightly flexed. He rubs his right foot slowly up and down the calf of his left leg as if polishing his shoe. The LaPunteda del Pie (foot tap) is another stalling device in which the free foot is tapped repeatedly against the floor. The lady can use the Pundeta while the gentleman is "shining his shoe", to show her irritation at being kept waiting.

Another corté, the Levantada, is orchestrated by the woman, who lifts her free foot and keeps her knees together, making the lower leg parallel to the floor. She then gently swings the free foot from side-to-side in an expectant gesture. Another variation, the Amague (a stamp or harsh tap), dramatizes frustration or indicates spirited moves ahead. The over-all spin on these variations is that they are employed as mediation devices to soften the rough edges in the man/woman relationship. The couple remains together throughout the "conflict" to solve relationship issues.

CORTÉ
In Business And In Life

Just as the partnership dynamics of the tango employ the corté to manage metaphorical tension, we also must manage tension or conflict at home and at work – for the sake of important relationships. Disruptions bring a halt to productivity, and must be addressed and resolved if defined goals are to be achieved successfully.

We often employ elaborate signals to communicate the tension we are experiencing. Just as dancers choose choreographed styling devices to telegraph their cortés, we use body language, key phrases, and habitual behaviors to let others know our displeasures, vulnerabilities and personal agendas. When these signals are sent, it is essential that businesses, families and friends honor mutual concerns and agreements.

Sometimes we must stop heading in directions which take us further from our goal. Throwing good money, time and resources after bad is poor judgment and can be disastrous if continued. Stopping to evaluate what has been done, to determine if it is activity or accomplishment, is an organizational corté; it is a necessary part of the process of working smarter, not harder. The value of a lifestyle corté is that it becomes the common-sense pause that refreshes relationships. This temporary cessation in frustration or open hostilities allows us to be more objective and analytical in resolving interpersonal conflicts.

TIP FROM YOUR COACHES: To resolve a conflict quickly, stop (corté) and evaluate the possible causes: Facts/Assumptions; Goals (what we should do); Processes (how we should do it); or Values/Beliefs. When confronting, always leave the other person an "out", so they can easily change their mind while saving face.

CUBAN MOTION

Cuban motion is a discreet, but expressive oscillating hip movement used in all rhythm and Latin dances. It is achieved by alternately flexing and straightening the knees with carefully-timed weight transfer. Without this highly stylized hip action, the rhythm and Latin dances would lose their flamboyance and sex appeal.

The Cuban motion defines the Latin mood and underwrites the attitude, form and function of all of the dances. It's what gives them the seismic quality that both liberates and checks the libido. Cuban motion is a celebration of the interconnectedness of body, mind and spirit as dancers express joy, beingness and life in the moment.

When you watch professional dancers execute cuban motion, it appears to be effortless. On the contrary, it is a movement that requires countless hours (make that years) of practice to perfect. The body is performing a movement that is unnatural and uncomfortable. However, once it is mastered, Cuban motion becomes a part of the body, mind and spirit of a dancer. As soon as the music begins, the Cuban motion moves into action.

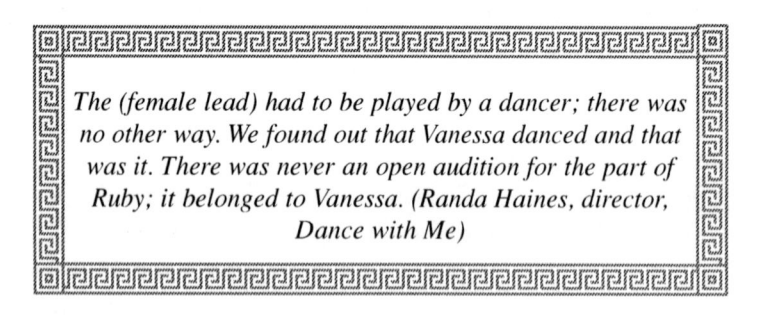

The (female lead) had to be played by a dancer; there was no other way. We found out that Vanessa danced and that was it. There was never an open audition for the part of Ruby; it belonged to Vanessa. (Randa Haines, director, Dance with Me)

CUBAN MOTION
In Business And In Life

Whenever we honor the "wait" transfer of energy and action between task completion and relationship development, we are moving in Lifestyle Cuban Motion. Tasks accomplished at the expense of work or social relationships leave us with a sense of emptiness.

The ability to manage the shift between work and relationships is not effortless. It requires as much passion, focus and practice as a good Cuban motion does for dance. It won't always feel comfortable – but once you have mastered it, you will never regret it.

Nothing robs teams more than producing a good product or service, but not feeling good about it because there was too much dissension and team conflict. Conceit and deceit rob social relationships of any chance to deepen and mature. We are deceived when we put work or selfish interests before mutually-satisfying human relationships.

The balance between human needs and work demands is Lifestyle Cuban Motion. If Lifestyle Cuban Motion is good and we believe we are valued as individuals as well as for our technical and financial contributions, we'll commit ourselves to productive work and social relationships. The fundamental message here is that the best teams, families and social relationships do not separate taking care of people and taking care of business. The Lifestyle Cuban Motion is a celebration of esprit de corps working in concert with living at the speed of life.

TIP FROM YOUR COACHES: Never sacrifice relationships for the sake of the bottom line. There is time to have both. It isn't always comfortable; it's never easy; but it is always worth the effort.

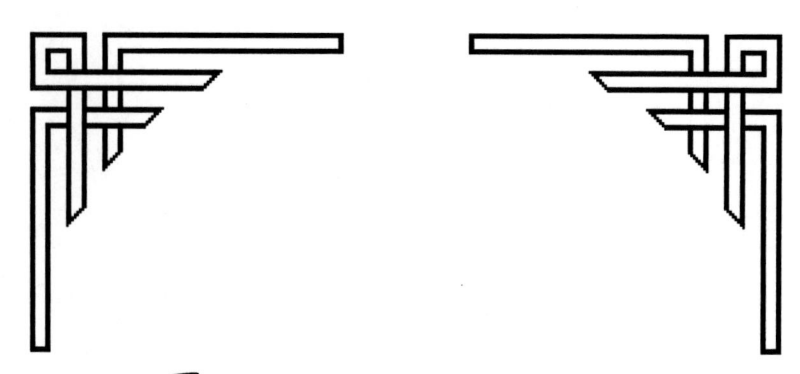

Two bodies united in the musical dash of veritable vivacity, feet twinkling in a unison of extraordinary alacrity, neuromuscular systems incredibly united, the thresholds of human dexterity are pushed to the limit.

(Frank Regan, former United States, Canadian and North American Champion; author of Championship Ballroom Dancing, The Year in Review, Dance Beat columnist, editor of International Dance Directory, and Director of the North American Dance Awards Production.)

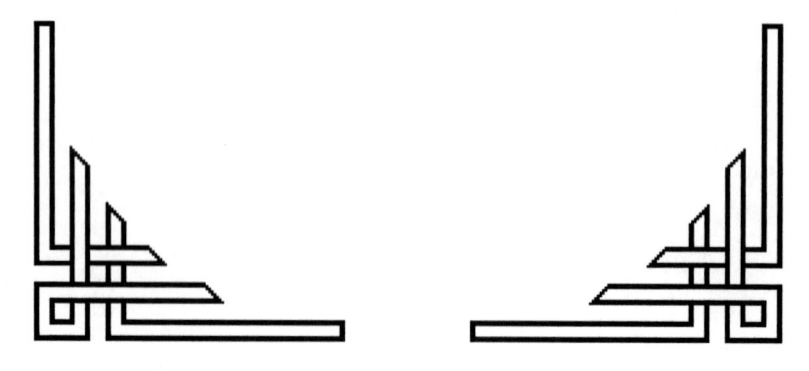

DANCE WISDOM
(Ask yourself: How do these quotes relate to my business and my life?)

I incorporated dancing into team meetings. Our project team had to develop a customized, in-house ...insurance applications program... We were under a lot of stress...so dancing helped us...build team spirit and have some fun.

(Phil Seyer, dance instructor, computer programmer)

I'm convinced that each time I dance, or even think about dancing, my immune cells get up and dance, too. I imagine them twittering among themselves about my passionate behavior and reaching a quick consensus that life is indeed worth living.
(Barry Sultanoff, M.D. holistic psychiatrist, ballroom dancer)

Most people think of dancing as a pebble at the beach, something that just anyone can pick up. But dancing is more like the precious pearl that lies at the bottom of the ocean. It takes work, study, and practice to search out that pearl and to bring it to the surface.

(Lauré Haile, world record-holder for ballroom pivots – 1 1/2 hours of non-stop turns)

Never satisfied until every detail is right, he will not compromise. How do you think those Astaire routines were accomplished? (There was) no loafing on the job in an Astaire picture...No sir... and no cutting corners.
(Ginger Rogers, legendary dancer)

DANCERS' EARS

The best ballroom dancers in the world possess what is known as "dancers' ears." When they hear a piece of music, it goes through their ears to their feet. They immediately think of ways of dancing to the rhythmic requirements of the music. They ask themselves, "Is it three-four time or four-four time? Is the cadence mixed, plagal (oblique) or suspended? Is its syncopation hot and jazzy or smooth and elegant? Are the lyrics strictly ballroom or can they be used for theatre arts routines? Is the music romantic, sensual or playful? Which dance patterns can we employ?"

Dancers' ears are constantly creating routines with every piece of music. New dance moves are not the products of text books. They evolve out of the dancer's experience—the way the dancer sees, feels, and hears the music. An ear for music is an awareness of life's joyful rhythms. And dance is about interpreting those rhythms through the physics of motion. Once you become a dancer, you never hear music in the same way again.

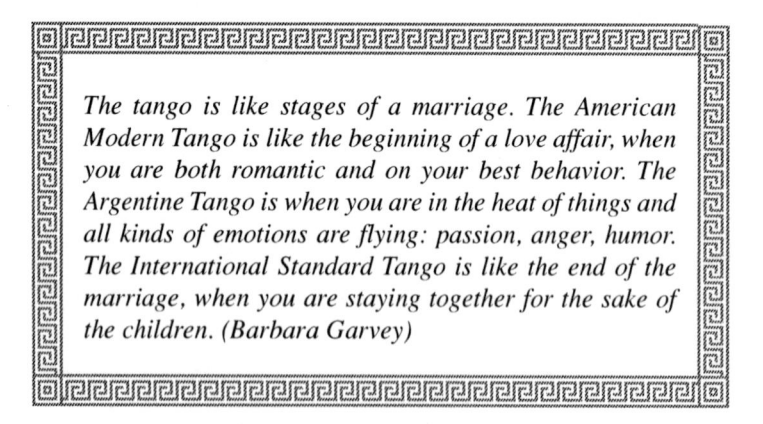

> *The tango is like stages of a marriage. The American Modern Tango is like the beginning of a love affair, when you are both romantic and on your best behavior. The Argentine Tango is when you are in the heat of things and all kinds of emotions are flying: passion, anger, humor. The International Standard Tango is like the end of the marriage, when you are staying together for the sake of the children. (Barbara Garvey)*

DANCER'S EARS
In Business And In Life

To develop successful partnerships, in business and in life, you must develop Dancer's Ears. This means you learn to listen beyond the words people say. So often we are not really listening to what someone is saying ... we are simply waiting for our turn to talk. Listening with Dancer's Ears requires you to really pay attention – not only to the words of the other person, but also to the implications, emotions and feelings being conveyed.

As you listen to others with whom you want to build strong partnerships, begin hearing the rhythm of the music. Are they sending joy or sadness; fear or confidence; hope or despair? What responses can you give that will be in sync with their needs? Teams, families or friends with Dancer's Ears know when a crisis is brewing and they are well aware of the difficulties associated with close relationships. The team's or family's survival depends on how well its members listen to each other and then get down to the business of cultivating productive relationships.

In resource-lean times teams and families alike must be able to hear the low guttural tone of sagging involvement and stagnation. With our "ears" on, we can learn very quickly how to anticipate changes in our social or organizational environments. We can create the conditions that make it possible for teammates and family members to use their lifestyle ears to prevent "hearing losses" or "tone deafness" to impair otherwise healthy relationships.

TIP FROM YOUR COACHES: Take time to listen to the "music" in your relationships at work and at home. Be sensitive to the subtle changes in tone, rhythm and behavior styles. Listen with the intent to understand!

EGO STATIC

Most of the dancers we have met, both professionals and amateurs, are wonderful people. But unfortunately there are those few who are extremely talented – and know it! In fact, they won't let anyone forget how good they are. This narcissistic behavior is what some dancers call ego static. It is usually accompanied by arrogance, conceit, self-importance and selfishness which usually make any and all contact with them an unpleasant experience. Ego static generally comes from performers who think they are God's gift to ballroom dancing. Their syrupy smiles, sanctimonious bromides and all-about-me conversations turn people off. Performance wise, they are rarely as good as they think they are and that makes them all the more difficult to coach – or appreciate. They seem to have a need for self-congratulation to prove their worth. These "victrolas" of conceit bring an edge of Velcro to any dance competition.

Ego static is particularly devastating in a dance partnership where one partner believes he or she is far superior to the other. Demanding and demeaning behaviors cut into the heart of the partnership, making it impossible to communicate clearly or create spontaneously. The resulting performance sends a message of unrest and frustration to judges and audience alike.

> *The key to successful collaborations is twofold: communication and not losing sight of the joy of working together. (Wynton Marsalis, first jazz artist to receive a Pulitzer Prize in music; and Peter Martins, Director N.Y. C. Ballet).*

EGO STATIC
In Business And In Life

Whenever you're around people, you've got to add their quirks, idiosyncrasies and personality flaws to the social mix. Most people are well-adjusted, hard-working, socially responsible, honest adults. Some seem to "hear the sound of a different drummer," but nevertheless are considered valuable members of teams as well as families. Invariably, however, there are those one or two narcissistic souls who erupt like pimples on otherwise smooth social relationships, causing frustration and resentment during their egocentric stay with the group.

Ego-obsessed people are the blood-ticks of private, business and social relationships. They sap the energy and add negative emotional energy wherever and whenever they park their attitude. The more ego static they generate, the more emotional sparks will fly, keeping everyone on edge and irritated. One of the best indexes to a team's or family's character is how well they manage out-of-control egos. High performance teams, whether they are business teams, ballroom dance teams, or family "teams" know how devastating narcissistic behavior is, and intervene as soon as possible to cut the ego static. Taking time to clarify and objectify goals, roles and responsibilities generally reduces or eliminates the static. Providing respectful feedback helps "altered" egos recover. If not, turn the window into a door and request the beleaguered egotist to "e-go" out the door.

TIP FROM YOUR COACHES: Create Key Operating Behaviors to establish boundaries within a partnership, then use them as a measure to keep ego static in check. Hold everyone involved in the partnership accountable, not only for the "what-to-do's," but also for the "how-to-do's."

EMOTIONAL GLUE

People are drawn to ballroom dancing competitions because competitive dancers' athleticism, theatrics and stamina are beyond most people's ability and comprehension. Dozens of couples loaded with talent mesmerize audiences with extraordinary choreography filled with twists, turns, and swirls that move souls. Competitive dancing at its highest level of excellence invigorates the spirits of those who watch, uniting the audience with the performers in an emotional language of mutual respect for excellence.

Audiences appreciate, and are often awed by the technical superiority of talented dance couples, but it is the emotional bonding between the genuinely engaged performers and the mesmerized audience that completes the "performance contract." Audiences expect technical expertise, otherwise the couple wouldn't be competing. It is the emotional glue that sells the couple's choreography to the audience and to the judges. A truly professional dance couple is invigorated not only by their shared pride in their dance partnership, but by the support of an inspired audience.

> *There's a quality (about dance) that's difficult to deal with in language...which is different from saying you can't describe dance in words...but you can reach all kinds of corners of the soul with language. (Martha Myers, Dean of the American Dance Festival)*

EMOTIONAL GLUE
In Business And In Life

Empathy is the emotional glue that holds relationships together. Take the "e" out of emotions, and you'll get "motions." Teams and families who just go through the motions miss one of the essential ingredients of relationship development – empathy – which is the ability to understand someone else's thoughts, feelings and circumstances. Tact, diplomacy, courtesy and politeness are all behaviors associated with empathy.

The emotional "geography" that affects all relationships can run hot and cold, smooth or rocky, calm or stormy, fertile or feudal. Ironing out psychological kinks and attitudinal knots are growing pains all teams and families go through. But truly productive business teams, families and social relationships stick together like glue when the going gets tough. They become 'connoisseurs of cool' in the midst of heated emotional environments, and turn emotionally-charged energies into engines of trust, respect and performance.

Teams and families that readily apply Lifestyle Emotional Glue create a chemistry that allows them to solidify relationships and amaze "outsiders" with their stick-to-it-iveness, stability and esprit de corps.

TIP FROM YOUR COACHES: Strengthen your Emotional Glue by practicing the art of paraphrasing: summarizing what you think you heard to your understanding. The sensitivity that results will create a lifestyle glue that adheres like an emotional epoxy, which strengthens the connections between team and family members alike.

FOCUS

Each member of the competitive dance couple must make a critical and conscious decision: Where is my focus in this performance? For whom am I dancing? Is it the steely-eyed judges? An admiring audience? My dance partner? Myself? My parents? My lover? My coach or dance studio? The ghost of Fred Astaire or Ginger Rogers? The media? To whom do I personally dedicate these adjudicated ninety-second performances?

Or do I dance for the thrill of dance itself? Is it the visible movement of an inner choreography? Is it a metaphor for my love of the arts ... an offering of my own uniqueness to others... a chance to demonstrate my talents... a need for recognition and validation? Who or what are the beneficiaries of my well-rehearsed chassés, multiple pivots and textbook dance frames?

Not only does each individual dancer make these crucial choices; both members of the partnership must have the same focus in mind. If one is dancing for the judges while the other is focused on the audience, an uneven performance (not to mention a rocky relationship) will result.

Technical matters aside, the dancer's relationship with the audience (the chief beneficiary of the dancer's performance) is an ethical matter. The couple's movements on the dance floor create the climate for innovative choreographies, tasteful seduction, and fan worship. But it can also "reel the audience in" to the full weight of the experience when the performers treat the audience as the primary beneficiaries of the extravaganza. Egos aside, the best dancers perform as much for the audience as for the prize money, recognition and awards.

FOCUS
In Business And In Life

For whom or what does your lifestyle bell toll? Where is your focus as you move through this ballroom called life? Until you can answer this question to your own total satisfaction, you will find yourself circling in eternal pivots and spins, often out of control and dissatisfied with the results.

Here are some of the complex questions that must be unraveled: For whom does a particular team or family member dance? Is it for steely-eyed project managers or in-laws? Hopeful customers or suitors? The member's protective spouse or sponsor? Resumé enhancement or social score card? A need for recognition and validation? A desire to show-off a particular talent or skill? Egos and hidden agendas aside, for whom should we dance and who are the beneficiaries of our talents, skills and commitments?

The purpose of effective relationships is to create efficient, harmonious, emotionally satisfying collective solutions to common problems. Effective teams, families and friends work together toward a common purpose, and like dance partnerships, want to excel and reap mutual benefits. Self-interest must give way to mutual interests. Individual goals must align with group objectives. The work at hand must always be more important than people's idiosyncratic differences. "Technical matters aside, (our) relationship with (others) is an ethical matter."

TIP FROM YOUR COACHES: Be sure everyone has the same vision of success—the same focus. Don't assume it...guarantee it! To guarantee you have the appropriate focus, determine your lifestyle first. Then wrap your work and relationships around that lifestyle.

GOTTA DANCE

The image of Gene Kelly, wearing a colorful jacket and singing "Gotta dance!" over and over again like a mini mantra contributed to the perception of competitive ballroom dancers as people obsessed with the performing arts. He symbolized the joyful exuberance of "hoofers" – regardless of the price they paid with sprained ankles, pulled muscles, beleaguered knees and social indifference in return for those few moments of glory and exhibitionism on the dance floor.

As an example of the unbelievable desire to dance at all costs, you might recall the vision of Gene Kelly in his famous rain scene from Singin' in the Rain. A little-known fact: when that scene was shot, Gene was wearing a heavy wool suit, soaked to the skin, and suffering from a serious cold. But you'd never know it from his signature smile and fancy footwork.

Like all clichés, there is an element of truth rooted in the expression "gotta dance", but clichéd or not, top performers in any discipline generally love what they do and gotta do it. They gotta dance, gotta write, gotta e-mail, gotta invent, gotta teach, gotta preach, gotta solve problems, gotta motivate, gotta…gotta…gotta!

Performers bitten by the "gotta bug" live by the motto: "Do what you love and success will follow." Although success means different things to different people, the bottom line is that people 'gotta do what they gotta do' to feel a sense of fulfillment and satisfaction. The real price they pay is not doing something they love. Doing something they find enriching is an investment that will pay lifelong dividends.

GOTTA DANCE
In Business And In Life

Gotta Dance – it's a cliché. But think about it. Clichés are expressions and ideas that have been used so often they've become a part of our common language. You can say the first few words, and just about anyone can finish the sentence. Some familiar survivors are: You can't teach an old dog new tricks; Better late than never; Work smarter, not harder; yada, yada, yada, and so on. Some clichés are filled with so much wisdom and uncommon sense that they have gained an air of reverence. A few examples of these best-in-class clichés are: We reap what we sow; What goes around comes around; Make love not war; Work hard, play hard; Know thyself; Cultivate an attitude of gratitude; Love thy neighbor as thyself; Do unto others; and Gotta Dance!

There's a reason why clichés become clichés – they hold kernels of truth. Try adopting the Gotta Dance cliché to spur team performance or family productivity. Identify what you all feel so strongly about that you can't NOT do it. People who are truly committed to defined goals possess the Gotta Dance attitude. Regardless of challenges, tight deadlines, unrealistic goals and interpersonal roadblocks, these "gotta" centered people keep their collective eyes on the goal. They constantly remind themselves and others that we gotta dance through life if we want to enjoy the journey.

TIP FROM YOUR COACHES: Perform a reality check on yourself and your partnerships. If money were no object, what would you be doing? Are you finding joy in what you do? How can you build a Gotta Dance commitment into all your partnerships? If you aren't finding joy in your work, you are paying much too high a price!

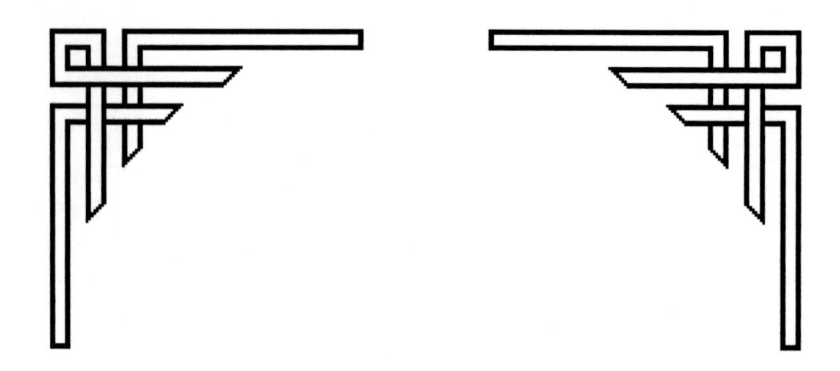

To be successful in a partnership, we need to be focused on the same goal, as well as being aware of our partner. Each one of us has to do our own job well, and mold ourselves together into one successful unit.

(Gregory Day, U.S. Theatre Arts & Cabaret Champion; British Open Exhibition champion; featured performer on PBS "Championship Ballroom Dancing")

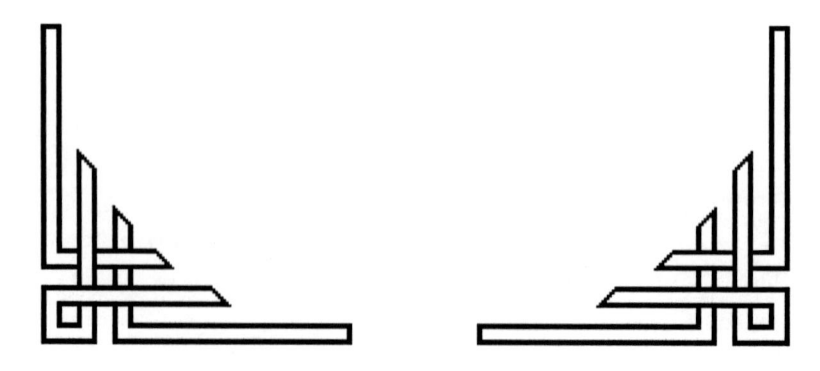

DANCE WISDOM
(Ask yourself: How do these quotes relate to my business and my life?)

Dancing may stimulate the release of body chemicals that act as a kind of fertilizer for nerve cells, slowing the death of brain cells that accompanies aging, preventing the connections between neurons from wasting away. Dancing may even produce a greater number of (neuron) connections.
(Informed Health Today magazine)

I see the globalization of culture as something positive. We should use all the nationalistic and regionalistic styles in the evolution of the arts.
(Paquito D'Rivera, band leader)

A study by the Sports Medicine Department of Friburg University showed that the effort exerted by DanceSport athletes in just one dance was equivalent to running 800 meters at a competition pace. The top DanceSport athletes usually have to dance thirty dances in a day of competitions, a major feat of endurance. NBC (might have) found the sport of the millennium to replace football.
(Peter Pover, Vice-President, International DanceSport Federation)

Dancing happens, dancing is always in the present.
(Peter Martins)

HARMONIC CONVERGENCE

Turns and circles are advanced moves which test a dancer's balance, control and respect for both centrifugal and centripetal forces. Although ballroom dancers use these two forces more than the average person, everyone has experienced the pull of gravity. For example, whenever you stand in one spot and whirl yourself around in a circle with your arms out wide, and feel the tingling sensation of blood rushing to your fingertips, you are experiencing centrifugal force. Centrifugal force is the thing that impels something or someone away from the center of rotation.

Centripetal force, on the other hand, counterbalances centrifugal push by pulling someone or something inward toward the center of rotation. Examples include motorcyclists leaning into the turn on a curve and track and field sprinters leaning into the turn in a race to maintain their speed, momentum and balance.

Dancers create exciting lines by creatively using these forces. We like to call the result Harmonic Convergence, because the result is achieved by the two dancers converging in harmony with one another.

This exaggerated centripetal and centrifugal forces can have obvious consequences if not done correctly, so dancers must be aware of the speed of rotation and the imaginary vertical axis that centers them for turns, spins and pivots. The partnership must provide the continuity of motion and necessary support to each other that gives turns and accelerated spins character, style and, most importantly, balance.

HARMONIC CONVERGENCE
In Business And In Life

Have you ever noticed how certain situations cause some people to fly apart, while others stand firm in the face of adversity? The difference is in the ability to apply emotional harmonic convergence: the ability to work in concert with those around us to control the gravitational pull of circumstances which affect us. We can either be pushed apart or pulled together depending on our choices – and our skills. Once you are on the competition floor, it is too late to begin practicing. The same is true in life. When problems, crises and issues hit, you must have the skills and partnerships you need to create harmonic convergence.

Centrifugal forces like jealousy, politics, token commitment, trust-erosion, accountability black holes, foggy roles and cloudy responsibilities can push people apart. Synergy is non-existent under these circumstances and rotation is away from core values. Centripetal forces, on the other hand, counterbalance negative attributes by pulling people cohesively toward core values.

When the push of individual weaknesses and personal agendas is counterbalanced by collective strengths and integrity, partnerships experience a harmonic convergence of talents, conscience and will. Lifestyle harmonics is the emotional "hub" of relationship development. The partnership axis is pointed toward true North because the atmosphere is one of reliability, sustainability and balance.

TIP FROM YOUR COACHES: Build strong networks of people who share your dreams and value you as a person. Use each other's strengths and counter-balance mutual weaknesses to achieve desired outcomes. None of us is perfect enough to carry the load by ourselves all of the time.

HEALTH INSURANCE

Dancers who come "on time" for dance lessons, coaching sessions or practice are already late. Serious ballroom dancers arrive twenty to thirty minutes early so they can warm up before the lessons or coachings begin. Adequate warm-up before practice sessions is a form of health insurance. Competitive ballroom dancing (DanceSport), like any sport, requires a warm, well-conditioned body. So proper warm-up is an extremely important health assurance factor.

Serious dancers apply the following health insurance premiums: They 1) stretch warm, well-worked muscles and never cold muscles. Stretching cold muscles is muscle abuse. 2) Hold a stretch for thirty to sixty seconds. Forcing or bouncing a stretch can cause ligament tears. 3) Stretch only to the point of mild discomfort, never beyond that. Stretching into pain is no gain—the damage is done. 4) Always sit or lie down to stretch. Stretching a weight-bearing muscle like a hamstring while standing is the kind of abuse that ends careers.

Stretching after a proper warm-up restores symmetry of alignment, which is particularly necessary after a tough practice, competition or performing a sequence that heavily emphasizes one body part over another. Failure to invest time and effort into these pre- and post- dance stretches will come back to haunt a dancer. It almost always leads to some type of debilitating injury in the future.

For dancers, the best insurance coverage they can "buy into" is the long-term policy called common sense. The pay out is a healthy body and a high degree of immunity from serious injury. The monthly insurance premiums are regular and consistent warm-ups, exercise and healthy nutritional habits.

HEALTH INSURANCE
In Business And In Life

Teams are a body of people with a shared purpose, working toward defined goals; families are the collective DNA of related bodies dancing around family trees. Both "bodies" are as healthy as the members allow – and like dancers, their health depends on their "pre- and post-performance stretches.

Pre-performance stretches include: establishing a common vision of success; clarifying roles and expectations; developing Key Operating Principles; identifying goals and processes; building trust, respect and camaraderie; and adding fun to the mix.

Post-performance stretches mean that those involved in the partnership, whether it be business, social or personal, make the time to assess how well they are doing. Reward and recognition for performance beyond the call of duty is essential. Celebration of success is a must.

Too often teams and families are so focused on the goals and activities that must be accomplished that they never take time to evaluate the process. They confuse activity with accomplishment. At the end of the day, they discover they have settled for unhealthy outcomes at the expense of strong, cohesive, healthy relationships.

TIP FROM YOUR COACHES: Just as dancers invest the time to warm up, getting their bodies ready for the strenuous activity to come, so must teams and families warm up to each other. Take time up front to clarify goals, roles and expectations. Don't forget the "cool down" – critiquing your progress and effectiveness at the end of every meeting or family gathering. And please, above all else: Celebrate Success! It's the best health insurance around.

IMPRESSION CONCESSIONS

During the standard dances, male partners move presidentially while wearing a set of tails, bow tie, stiff plastic collar and waist vest. Even though male dancers express characteristic emotions during the competitive performance (confident, playful joy during the Foxtrot and quick step, romantic delight in the Waltz, or detachment during the Tango) their carriage remains consistently textbook.

The female role in this competitive twosome is decidedly different. The women wear exquisitely designed gowns which emphasize and exaggerate the couple's choreographed moves. The women's faces are radiant and framed with sparkling jewels; their sometimes outlandish hair-do's complement the occasion. Tanned bodies, long fingernails and glamour-length eye lashes add to the mystique. For the women, all must be gaiety and lightness, all movement must appear spontaneous and effortless despite ankles and knees which scream in protest, calves which knot into cramps and spike- heeled pumps which squeeze like a mammogram machine for the toes.

The couple ignores the inherent discomforts associated with their attire and performance, and opts instead to amp-up their showmanship to mesmerize the judges and fans alike. The vocabulary of dancing is defined by the couple's ability to manage impressions, using every cubic foot of the dance floor as they spin and whirl past competitors with apparent comfort, joy and abandon.

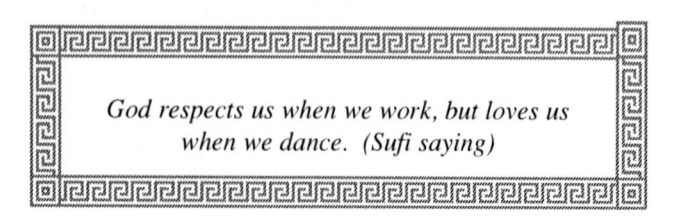

> *God respects us when we work, but loves us when we dance. (Sufi saying)*

IMPRESSION CONCESSIONS
In Business And In Life

Effective partnerships, despite their faults, flaws and follies, manage to present a professional image to colleagues, friends and customers alike. Success depends on being good at impression management. Effective teams and families both have a knack for concealing smirks, smears and smudges in order to present a good appearance to the outside world.

Public movements must appear "spontaneous and effortless," despite members' frustration with unreasonable demands and limited resources which knot a team's or family's financial muscles or emotional flexibility into cramps. Teams, families and best friends can persevere by tolerating discomforts and accepting human idiosyncrasies as the social costs associated with close relationships.

Business people know that customers do not want to hear about the internal problems of the service provider. Customers want results, not excuses. The team that projects a winning image while it meets or exceeds customer expectations is the team that keeps its internal confessions and concessions to itself. Families know the value of keeping skeletons in closets and difficulties under wraps, so they can protect themselves from the slings and arrows of society.

TIP FROM YOUR COACHES: Dancers learn very early in their professional careers that judges and audience alike want to see the movement, not the effort behind the movement. We must also realize that customers, top management, relatives and friends want to see enthusiastic, "effortless" results. Keep the pain and agony to yourself. Deal with it 'behind the scenes' with the help of trusted confidants.

IMPROVISATION

Every competitive ballroom dance consists of strict rules about how the steps are to be performed, which cover the gamut from head to toe. With such intense established parameters, you would think everyone dancing a certain dance would look the same. Not true! Competitive couples use their own freedom of expression and special choreography to augment their dance performance. But true dancing genius springs from the interaction of the competitors' free spirits as they ad lib off one another to respond to unexpected situations. This sudden improvisation—unscripted, unpredictable and unrehearsed—adds spontaneous variation to a routine performance.

We have seen couples actually collide with other couples, then turn the collision into such a creative pose that one is left wondering if the "meeting" was part of the choreographed routine. That is creative improvisation!

Improvised moves also occur during closed syllabus competitions even though there is less wiggle room. When the dance floor is crowded with competitors, couples must maneuver through the maze without compromising their floor craft or dance frames. Couples who begin a sequence of syllabus-driven dance moves across the floor must be on the alert for possible "interference" by competing couples who have launched their own movement. Redirection, ad libs and cortés (sudden stops) are common as couples strive to orchestrate required patterns while avoiding collisions with other couples.

Quick thinking and improvisation are necessary tools for the competitive ballroom trade. Even in social ballroom dancing, crowded floors demand awareness, timing and improvisation from pre-occupied couples who put more spin in conversation than in the line of dance.

IMPROVISATION
In Business And In Life

Improvisation in business and in life refers to the uncanny ability to dance around bothersome personalities, skill deficiencies and attitudinal black holes with apparent ease and grace. Teams and families with highly developed improvisational skills can "ad lib" off difficulties and turn problems into solutions faster than a hotly-contested jitterbug. Their penchant for wiggle room, using hunches and intuition, generates a "special choreography" of their own as they search for connections, similarities and polarities related to the problem at hand.

For high velocity teams, work itself is improvisational theater. It is a stage for team members' collective creativity, ingenuity and interests. Equipped with patience, playfulness and passion, they see organizational problems as auditions which showcase their ability to "trip the light fantastic" around worrisome organizational issues. Families can be just as adept at solving kinship issues. Success in business and in life comes from a highly evolved ability to think on your feet, and respond appropriately, quickly and with a sense of humor. We call this skill "Lifestyle Improv."

Tip From Your Coaches: Build improv skills by periodically playing relationship development games that require quick thinking, fast changes, and responsiveness to individual and group needs. A good one: Have someone ask a question, then answer it as a group, with each person adding one word at a time. You'll be amazed at the results, as well as the increased skills in listening.

GRAND JETÈ

One of the most exciting dance moves is borrowed from ballet. Called the Grand Jetè, this movement occurs when a dancer, in full flight, leaps into the air into a full airborne split. The dancer appears to fly across the floor, in an expression of exuberant joy and excitement.

A good dancer makes this move look easy, graceful and exciting. As we attempted to learn this move, we discovered that looks can be very deceiving! In reality, the Grand Jetè requires immense effort, flexibility and control, along with split-second timing.

The Grand Jetè is used in choreography to emphasize a high point in the music—a climax of emotion and joy. It takes years to perfect, but continues to be one of the mainstays in choreographed routines.

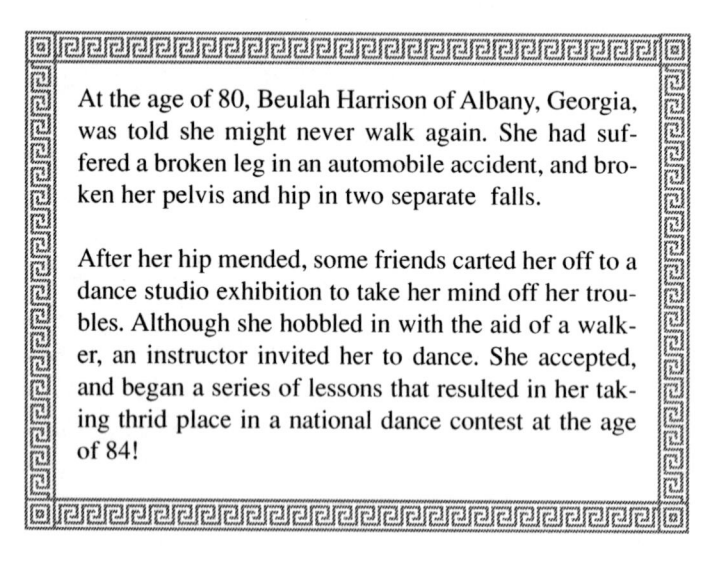

At the age of 80, Beulah Harrison of Albany, Georgia, was told she might never walk again. She had suffered a broken leg in an automobile accident, and broken her pelvis and hip in two separate falls.

After her hip mended, some friends carted her off to a dance studio exhibition to take her mind off her troubles. Although she hobbled in with the aid of a walker, an instructor invited her to dance. She accepted, and began a series of lessons that resulted in her taking thrid place in a national dance contest at the age of 84!

GRAND JETÈ
In Business And In Life

There are moments in our life that require celebration—big celebration. When stretch goals are achieved, we need to use the Grand Jetè principle to express our satisfaction and the joy of accomplishment.

In today's highly-accelerated work environment, we are often asked to perform impossible tasks in unrealistic time frames. In our personal lives, we try our best to keep our family relationships and friendships solid and loving in the midst of chaos and change. When we meet our goals, when we successfully balance our work and personal lives, we have beaten the odds—we've won another lifestyle battle between making a living and living a life.

Too often we take our successes for granted. When things go wrong, we spend an inordinate amount of time assessing blame, beating ourselves up, and analyzing what to do next. But when things go right, what happens? Nothing. We plod on to the next challenge. We need to take time to celebrate our accomplishments. . . reinforce our successes.

Lifestyle Jetès are leaps for joy on the stage of life, celebrations of spirit over matter. They are visible demonstrations of our ability to rise above the routineness and mundaneness of life.

TIP FROM YOUR COACHES: Reward successes by having "Grand Jetè" celebrations that recognize efforts that require special collective skill collaboration, timing and effort. Use a prominent bulletin board to publicize your Grand Jetè Announcements, recognizing achievements and successes. Be bold in celebrating your accomplishments.

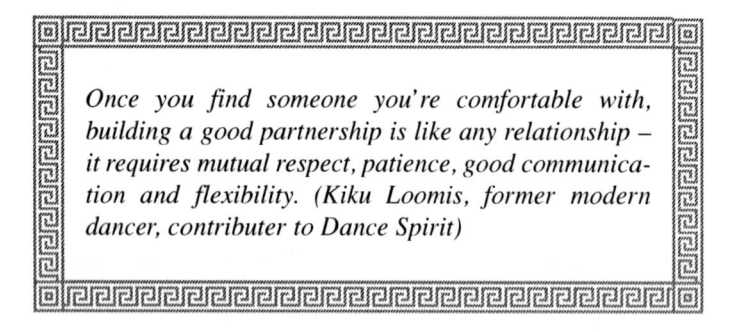

JUNK REHEARSAL

World class ballroom dancers go full out in rehearsals. They do not compromise the integrity of any workout. Dancers who are serious about dance know how important practices are because they believe preparation is everything.

Serious competitors know that perfect practices lead to perfect competitive performance and junk practices produce lackadaisical attitudes that lead to performance garbage.

Championship DanceSport athletes make time in rehearsal to simulate problems that might occur. By developing a comfort zone in handling potential disasters, such as missed cues, trip-ups, forgotten material or interference from other couples, dancers can walk onto the floor with confidence and poise. They know that perfect rehearsals are the breakfast of dance champions.

> *Once you find someone you're comfortable with, building a good partnership is like any relationship – it requires mutual respect, patience, good communication and flexibility. (Kiku Loomis, former modern dancer, contributer to Dance Spirit)*

JUNK REHEARSAL
In Business And In Life

Individuals who are truly successful in business and in life know the secret of going full-out in "rehearsals". They understand that preparation is the key to a powerful performance, whatever the situation. There is compelling evidence to suggest that when we attend one-shot "mountain-top" classroom sessions, sit passively at the feet of content gurus, waiting for that flash of wisdom, and refuse to take learning seriously, the quality of our "real world" experience suffers. Not to be fully present in life experiences is planned emotional obsolescence and dampens our joy and appreciation for the fullness of life.

The partnership between willing student and life situation guarantees that learning can take place. Outcomes can be seen as lessons, and future contexts can be viewed in relationship to past experiences when we learn to take advantage of life's class rooms.

We know that each life experience is a dress rehearsal for the next life experience. We learn that guarantees are counterfeit experience. We cheat ourselves if we eliminate risk and uncertainty. Our "schooling" becomes lifestyle junk if it's risk-free, emotionally unexciting, intellectually bankrupt, physically undemanding and spiritually numbing. We learn that life is not a spectator sport. It is high-contact, full-out, unadulterated living at the speed of life-changing experiences.

TIP FROM YOUR COACHES: Live life full-out – or as full-out as you can. Welcome the unknown, but prepare for it. Use role playing, test runs, debriefings and family conferences to arm yourself for a great performance.

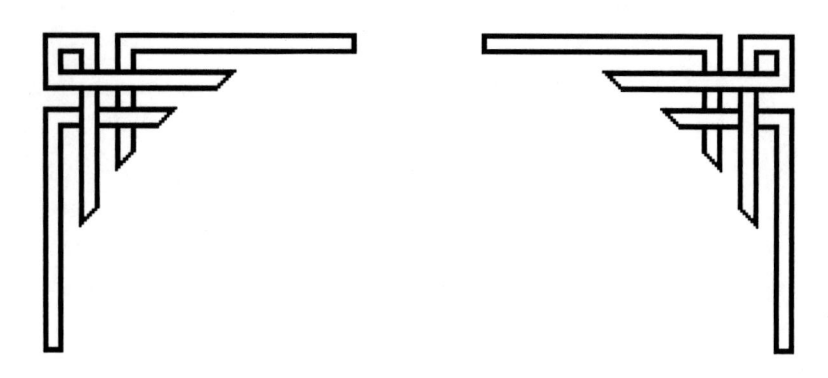

I discovered a wonderful quote from a book entitled <u>Fear Not</u>, which could apply to the gift we have been given — dance. It says: 'Styles and choreography change ... but the fundamental principles remain unchanged.' This is so true in this fast paced world of today.

(Bill Sparks, United States Latin Champion and World Finalist)

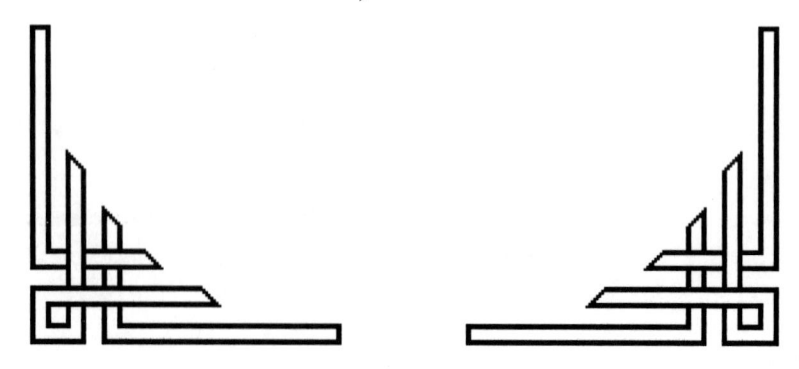

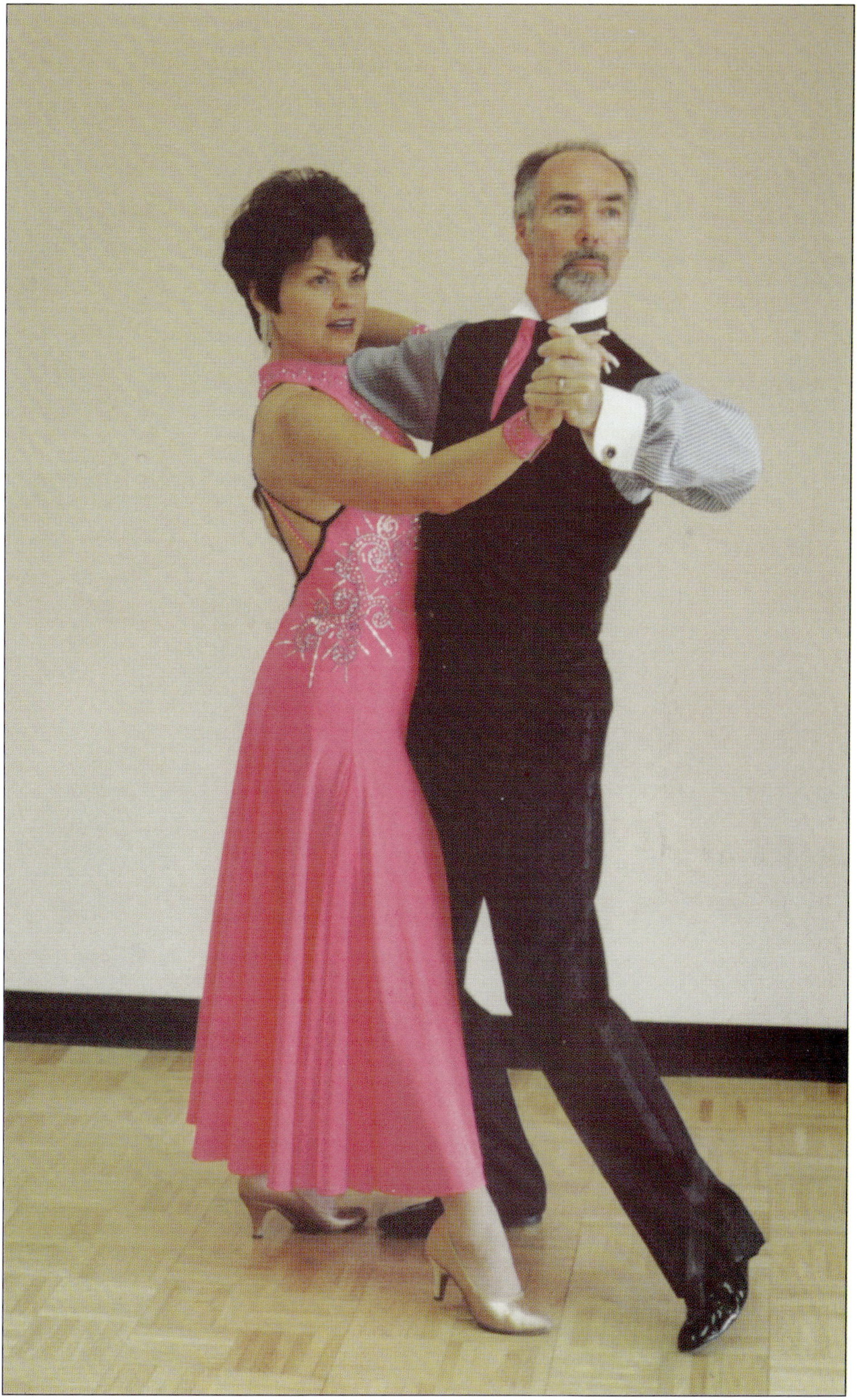

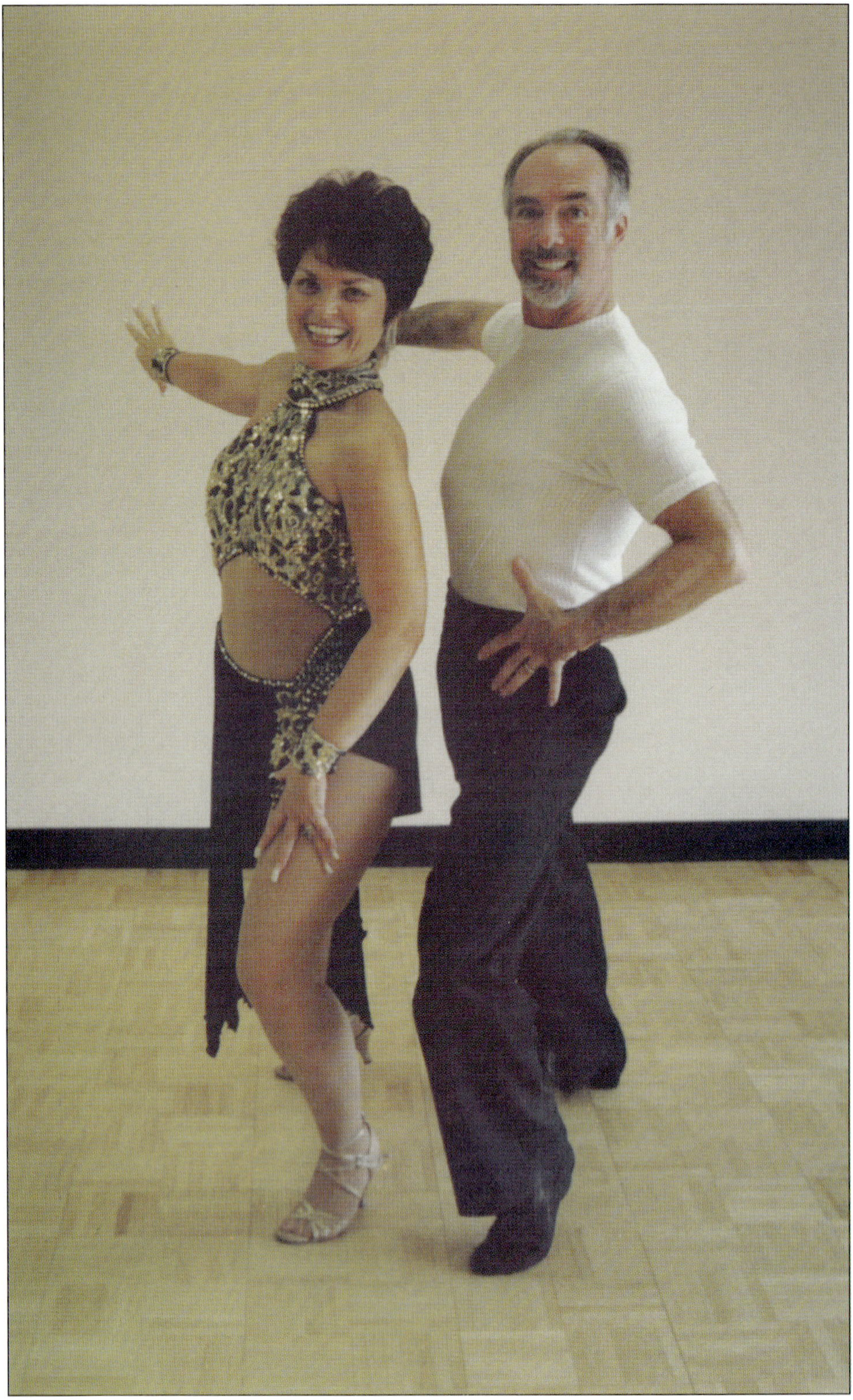

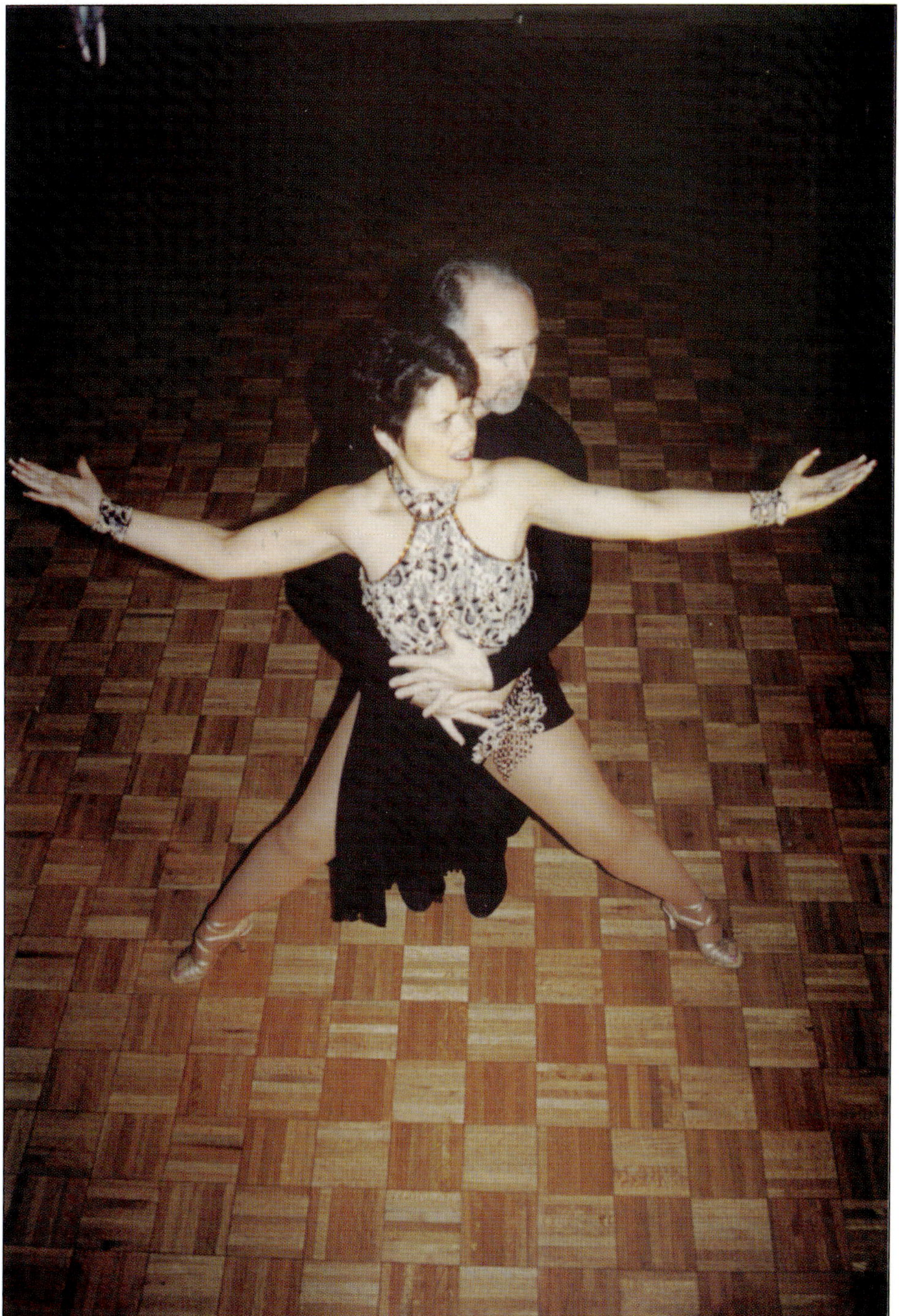

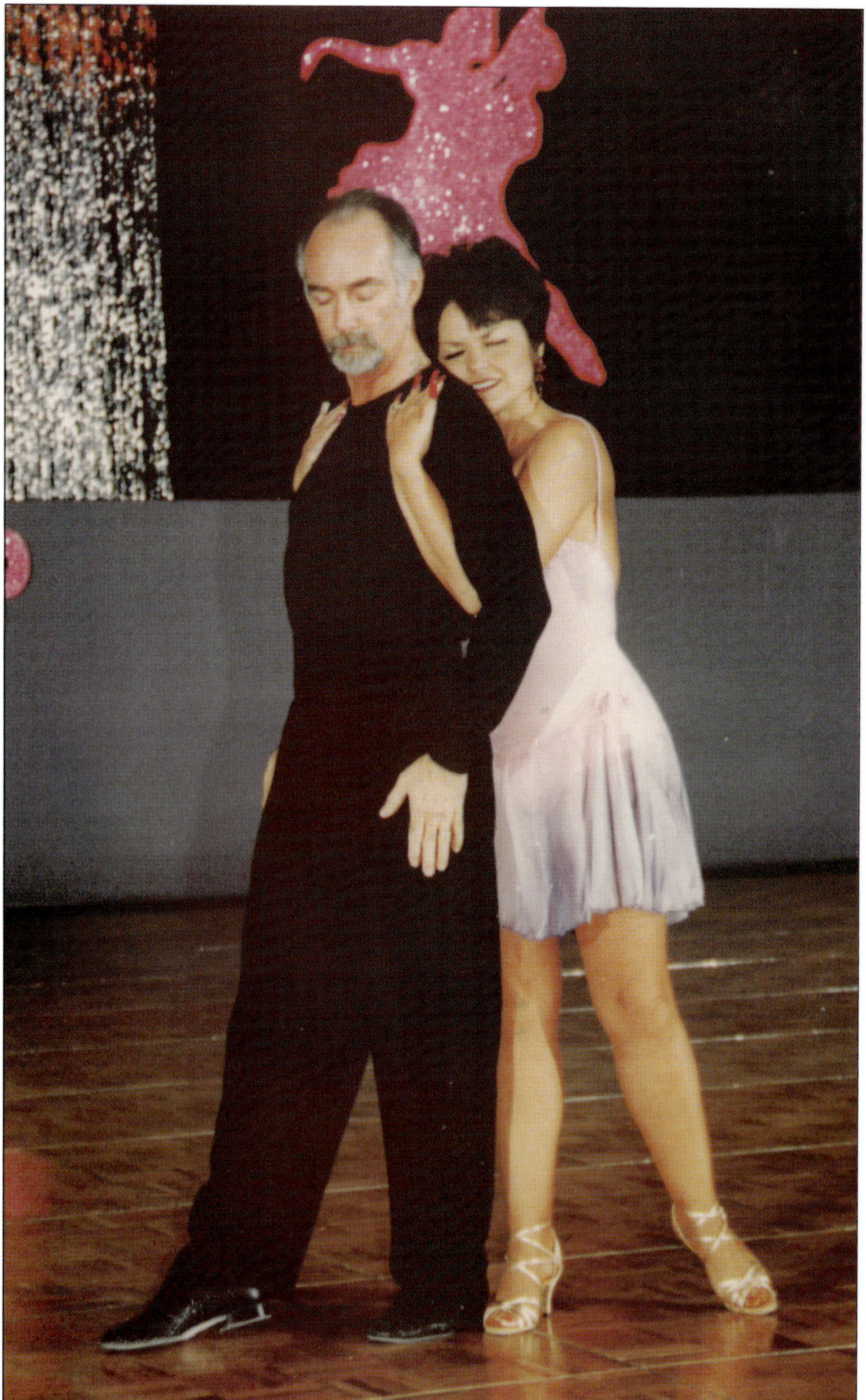

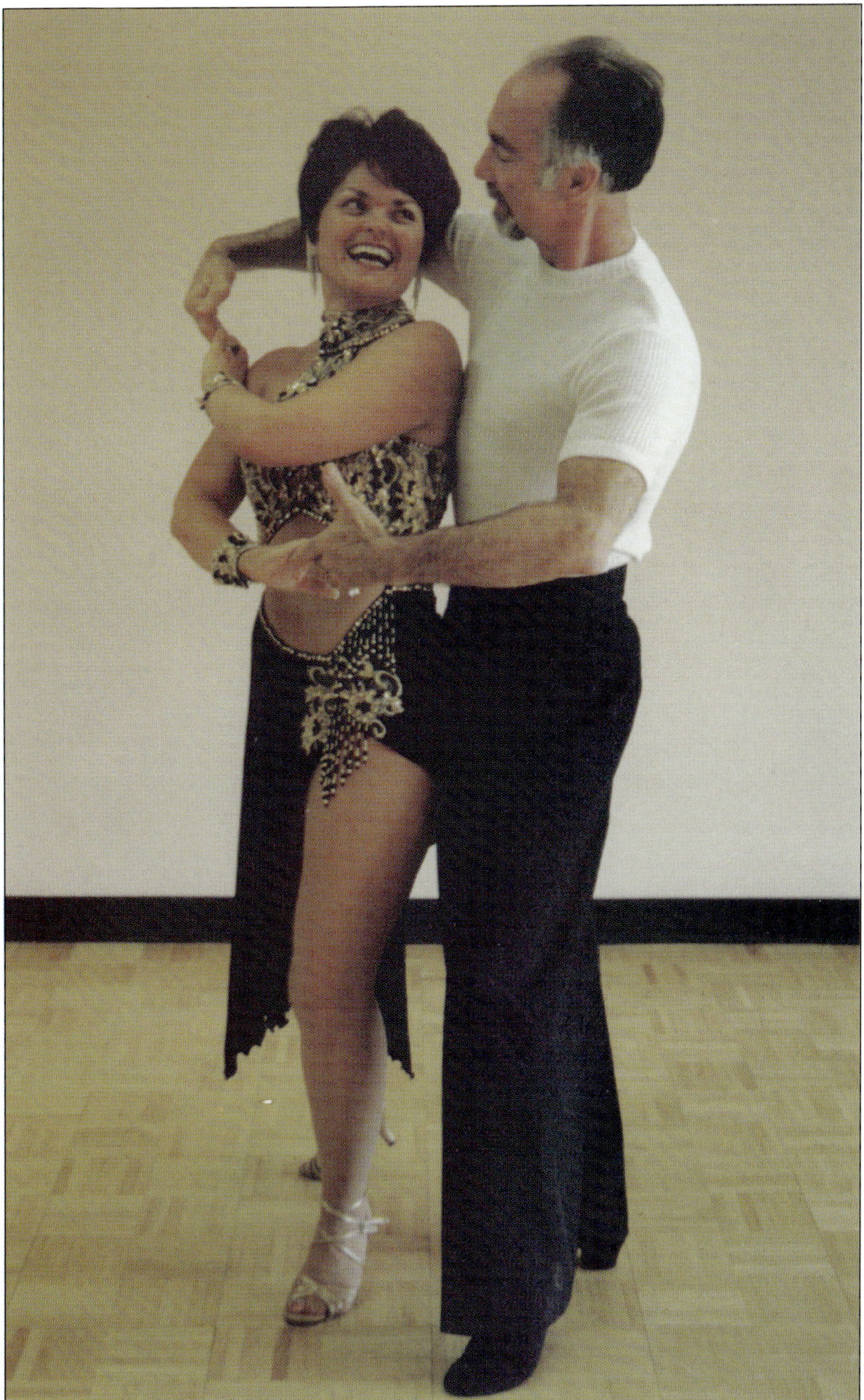

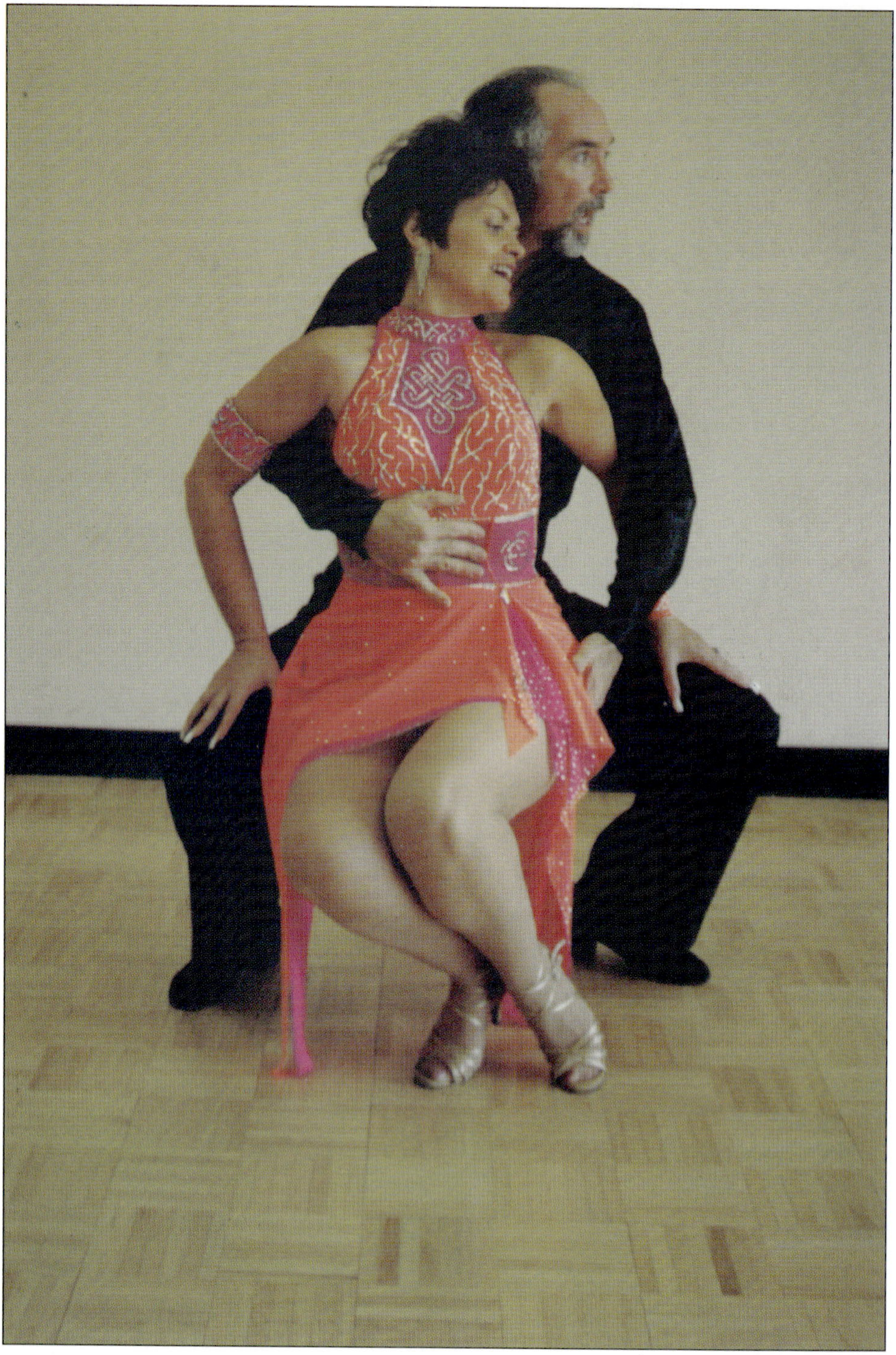

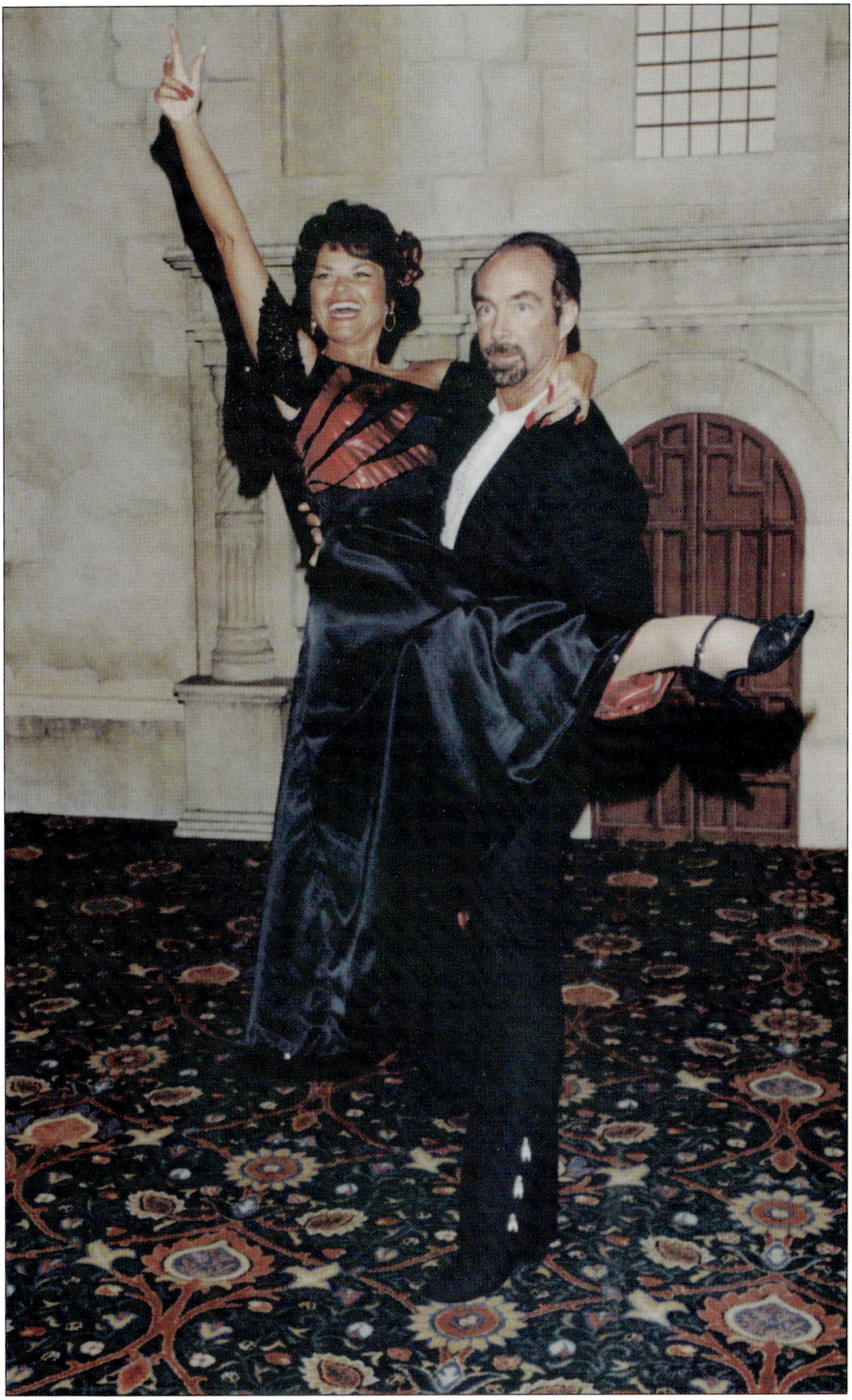

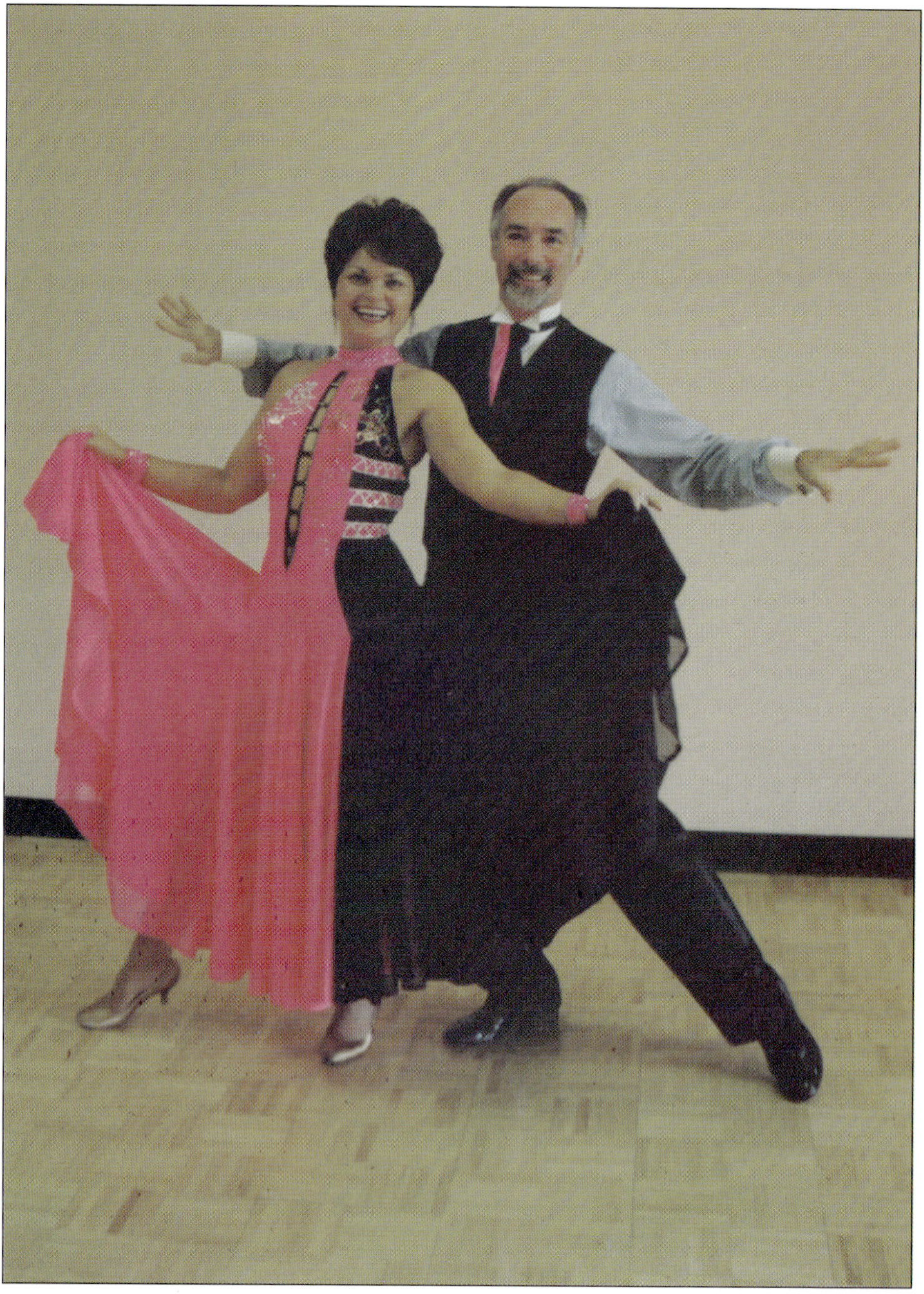

DANCE WISDOM
(Ask yourself: How do these quotes relate to my business and my life?)

Quitters are not born, they are trained. Give (dancers) life lessons at every turn.
(Kathryn Austin, director in dance
and the performing arts)

The musicality learned in tap is greatly helpful in other forms of dance. When students (become) aware of the rhythms inherent in dance, they have what I (call) an "inner metronome." This means that no matter where they are in the choreography, they instinctively know the count.

(Stephanie Lawton, former Rockette)

I would like to sit under a tree, drink wine, and watch people dance.
(Adlai Stevenson)

The arms of American trained dancers are not considered worthy of comment by most of the European community....The fingers have digits which can fold and open to reveal emotion and musicality and finish the beautiful lives in the (arabesque) position.

(Peff Modelski, dance critic, theatrical consultant)

KUDO KUDZU

Every performer loves recognition in the form of kudos and awards. Peer and public acknowledgement for superior performance has been a motivator since people first organized themselves into groups thousands of years ago. Some type of special remuneration for outstanding service to a club, city, community or country has helped people establish themselves as the best, fastest, strongest, smartest and busiest people on earth.

Kudos, awards and pay are the chief differentiators of the favored few over the admiring many. Higher prize money and global media coverage are forcing dancers to follow public tastes and ballroom judges' idiosyncratic appetites. Dizzying spins, aggressive aerials, selfish panhandling of floor space, provocative moves and exotic costuming are influencing some judges at dance competitions. DanceSport couples are opting for the pay, perks, prestige and power associated with showmanship and glitz – often at the expense of technically correct dancing.

The challenge competitors face is to keep the championship trophies, titles, awards and kudos in perspective. Ballroom dancing is a performing art, and turning it into a business has its drawbacks. When dance competitors dance just for the camera or perform only for awards, they run the risk of giving up too much of themselves and their talents. The focus has changed, and they are letting kudo kudzu take over. Ego, like fast growing kudzu, can squeeze the life out of everything around it, leaving superficiality instead substance. Public approval, power and awards become weeds that can choke the life out of the dance.

KUDO KUDZU
In Business And In Life

Everyone enjoys recognition. But sometimes the awards and honors overshadow the very performances we are recognizing. Somewhere in the process of rewarding performance, we create a whole new business – how to get the prize.

Business and industry offer quality improvement honors like the Malcolm Baldridge Award. The entertainment industry awards Oscars, Emmys, Tonys, etc. Community service organizations offer appreciation such as the Jefferson Award. The National Collegiate Athletic Association awards the Heisman Trophy. Civic organizations offer plaques as appreciation for superior volunteerism. Families throw parties and buy gifts for the anointed. Tangible recognition for a job well done is something people come to expect from those they serve.

Our challenge is to keep awards, fancy titles, and kudos in perspective. Excessive glitz and recognition undermine performance when people focus on the prestige power of the award and lose sight of what the award stands for. Politics creep in, and the business of winning takes precedence over the performance. Counterfeit achievement usually leads to a progressive degradation in the quality of everything represented by the award. When awards become political, recognition is usually more bogus than real. Losing faith in public recognition causes kudos to become kudzu, and feelings of dissent, cynicism and betrayal creep into the awards ceremony.

TIP FROM YOUR COACHES: Evaluate your reward and recognition process. Be sure appropriate behavior is being rewarded, and that recipients feel the awards are legitimate.

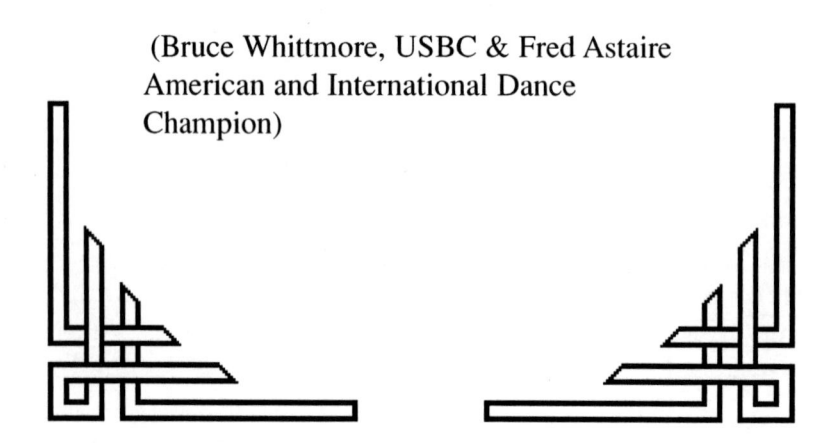

Dancing and corporate business...both work at assimilating ideas and composing them into common goals. Both require discipline, timing, direction, individual involvement with expression and motivation to create a sensitive partnership.

(Bruce Whittmore, USBC & Fred Astaire American and International Dance Champion)

DANCE WISDOM
(Ask yourself: How do these quotes relate to my business and my life?)

Dance is the landscape of the soul.
> (Martha Graham, legendary performing arts dancer and choreographer)

Dance, even when dressed in its richest costumes and most sophisticated techniques, never loses its connection with gut reality. (F. Borrows)

It's no fun to dance with someone who dances all over your feet. Picking partners with common rhythms, goals, and values is crucial. You can't have one partner doing the tango and the other dancing the waltz. You will wind up dragging each other all over the floor.
> (Jack Dowling)

Dance is...an international language which every human being is able to understand — and it should be used as such.
(Rudi van Dantzig, choreographer)

LEADING

A great deal of misleading talk is tossed around these days about the concept of leading in ballroom dancing. Proper leads, contrary to conventional propaganda, do not involve gentlemen shoving ladies into particular dance patterns or moves. A good strong lead from the gentleman merely makes clear his intention to the lady, who then completes the move, pattern or figure. A proper lead is essentially a well-timed non-verbal cue from the gentleman which indicates a change in direction or intent based on factors such as choreography, the availability of floor space and/or positioning of other dancers.

In DanceSport, the lady as well as the gentleman knows all of the dance patterns and choreography, so she doesn't have to be forced into a move. Strong leads are not macho power moves. The gentleman doesn't have to herd the lady into a movement according to his whims. Force is not leading. It is confrontation, and confrontation produces combativeness – whether it occurs on the dance floor or work floor.

The secret to a good lead is the gentleman's ability to maintain a consistent frame, while initiating the particular pattern he is leading his partner into next. Done correctly, there is no question or confusion in his partner's mind as she completes the movement with beauty, poise, expression and energy.

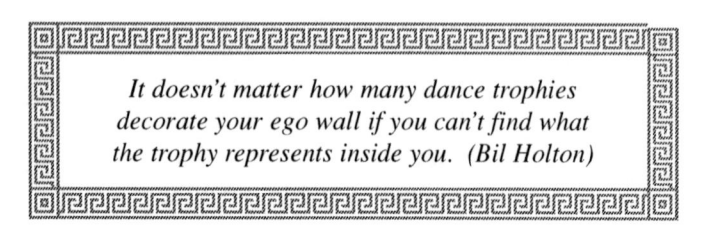

> *It doesn't matter how many dance trophies decorate your ego wall if you can't find what the trophy represents inside you. (Bil Holton)*

... in business and in life

LEADING
In Business And In Life

The efficiency of the leader is the efficiency of the led. True leadership – in business and in life – is the ability to galvanize people's wills and energies and to transform the leader's vision into practical, cost effective, enduring reality. The leader's role is to indicate the big picture, then allow talented people to "complete" the masterpiece to the best of their abilities. Leadership, on the work floor, in the living room or on the the dance floor, is about establishing a sense of direction. Once direction is established through believable vision, mission and values, the leader's role is to eliminate obstacles that interfere with transforming the vision into reality.

A strong lead (clarified vision, mission, goals, roles and values) is the only "push" people need. The leader's intentions are ratified when those doing the work accomplish desired outcomes. The important thing to remember is that "leading" is not participative management — it is managing participation. And "completing" what is begun is not the same thing as following, since followership is based on blind obedience to established rules and authority, while completing is based on reaching the same conclusions and acting in concert with shared values, beliefs and work methods. Completing is an equity arrangement, following is based on perpetuating inferior relationships.

TIP FROM YOUR COACHES: As you work in any partnership, be sure the message you send in terms of vision, values, goals and expectations is clear, and consistent with your behavior. Mixed messages lead to confusion, distrust, disinterest, and poor performance.

LEOTARDS AND PIROUETTES

Good dancers watch their weight—because they know they can't fool anyone when they're wearing tights. Ounces become unsightly pounds under a leotard. Any extra weight is noticed by the audience, competitors and judges. World-class ballroom dancers have to stay in shape and watch their weight because the competitions are merciless. The level of competition requires competitors to dance through repeated heats, quarter-finals, semi-finals and championship rounds before the competition is complete. The rigorous competition can take all evening—to the delight of the audience, but to the exhaustion of the athletes.

The thin "look" applies to both men and women. It's a burden both members of the dance couple share. Each ballroom couple, whether they compete in smooth or rhythm, standard or Latin, or in cabaret, must pay critical attention to their combined health. Diet, nutrition and exercise are high priorities, not only for maintaining the "look," but for strong, healthy, competitive bodies.

It has been said that the famous ballet master, Mikhail Baryshnikov was very strict about the weight of the ballerinas with whom he danced. If he felt they had gained weight, he would let them know by uttering an "umph" as he lifted them into the air. Ballroom dancers may be a bit more subtle, but extra pounds does affect the look of both the dancer and the dance.

Whenever ballroom dancers, particularly theatre arts competitors, prepare for up-coming competitions, they ask themselves: How will I look in leotards during pirouettes? If the answer is a few pounds too heavy, they add extra conditioning workouts to an already full competitive schedule.

LEOTARDS AND PIROUETTES –
In Business And In Life

Highly successful businesses and families recognize the need to be "lean and mean" when it comes to managing wants and necessities. We're not talking about body fat here. The "thin look" we are referring to means purposefully and consistently trimming excess "fat" like excuses, hidden agendas, role confusion, irresponsibility, unproductive meetings or gatherings, and so on. Lifestyle "fat" is anything excessive that interferes with satisfying and productive relationships.

Lifestyle pirouettes is a phrase you can use to describe successful "exercising" that keeps your team's or family's "achievement muscles" in shape. It means living and working with the philosophy that all excess is excess. For families and businesses alike, lifestyle pirouettes are used as barometers to avoid the physical, mental and material excesses that strain relationships.

If you want to "look good in the leotards of life", you have to prepare ahead of time. The day of the performance is too late to begin exercising. It takes a lot of work to be able to work together effectively as a work team or a family. Do what it takes to prepare, so that when "showtime" hits, you can hit the floor running!

TIP FROM YOUR COACHES: Constantly ask yourself "How would I look in a leotard doing a pirouette?" In other words, are you in sync, free of excuses, prepared to hit the floor running? If not, take action – even in the midst of an unrealistically busy schedule. Do some lifestyle conditioning.

LINE OF DANCE

Have you ever wondered how competitive ballroom dancers keep from running into one another as they glide, pivot and grapevine across the floor? One principle that help them is the Line of Dance. The Line of Dance represents an imaginary line drawn counter-clockwise around the ballroom floor. It is the direction of the dance, the line of progression which all dancers travel with their partners to establish some semblance of order. The wall is on the gentleman's right and the center of the floor is on the gentleman's left.

The line of dance only applies to the travelling dances — Waltz, Foxtrot, Tango, Viennese Waltz, Quickstep and Paso Doble. The Rhythm and Latin dances are generally parochial dances (spot dances), although in DanceSport competitions couples may travel completely across the floor to "unwind" their choreographed routines.

Without a conceptual line of dance to serve as a directional medium, the dance floor would be a chaotic and confusing conglomeration of spinning bodies and colliding couples.

In the midst of highly technical and sophisticated dance moves, one of the constants that couples count on is Line of Dance.

> Just try and keep up with those feet of his sometimes! Try and look graceful while thinking where your right hand should be and how your head should be, and which foot you end the next eight bars on…not to mention those Astaire rhythms.
> (Ginger Rogers, legendary dancer)

LINE OF DANCE
In Business And In Life

Agreed upon key operating principles help teams as well as families stay on the "same page" or in the "line of dance." Without a clearly defined lifestyle line of dance, our environment can be a chaotic and confusing conglomeration of spinning technologies and colliding personalities that turn well-rounded teamwork into a not-so-merry-go-round.

When we work with clients to develop values and Key Operating Principles, we use a simple but powerful activity to drive home the importance of "Line of Dance". We show a slide filled with arrows pointing in different directions. As we point to each arrow, the group must move in that direction while loudly saying the direction in which they are moving. We then ask them to say what they see on the slide, but move in the opposite direction. The result is funny, but chaotic – as people run into one another in a mass of confusion. We then switch it, so they do what they see while saying the opposite. The results are similar. We wrap up the exercise by having everyone enthusiastically doing and saying what they see. The result drives home the importance of congruence between what you value, what you say, and what you do.

Just as dancers depend on the Line of Dance, so must we rely on the consistency of our vision, values and goals. This brings a sense of order to the challenging responsibilities we face in the 21st Century.

TIP FROM YOUR COACHES: In your partnerships, develop clearly defined and agreed-upon Key Operating Principles. When you "crash into each other", evaluate behaviors against agreed-upon principles to get back into the 'Line of Dance.'

METERED TIME

Meter describes the number of beats in a measure of music. For example, a Foxtrot is danced in 4/4 time. There are 4 beats to a measure of Foxtrot music. This meter remains the same no matter what type of Foxtrot is played. Waltzes, both the slow and Viennese, are danced in three beats per measure, with the emphasis on the first beat. Metered time makes it easy to tell the duration of a movement by counting the number of beats in each measure.

The rate of speed of the metered beat may change, but the number of beats remains constant. All competitors dance to the same time standard, so it is easy to see who is on or off beat. Sometimes dancers add chassés or settle into the beats to augment the established rhythm or to execute a particular move, but the metered beat stays the same.

The "metered time" provides an agreed-upon structure, within which competitors create their unique choreography. We've observed dance couples who have fabulous tricks to flaunt their skills, but their timing is off beat. While they strut their stuff proudly, the judges are marking them down and turning to look at other dancers, who may not be as flashy, but understand the timing of the dance they are performing.

Competitors who are "off-beat" automatically lose points with the judges, because being "on-beat" is a non-negotiable technical requirement. Dancing off-beat is like raking one's fingernails across a chalk board. It causes judges to cringe – figuratively and literally.

METERED TIME
In Business And In Life

Our personal and professional code of ethics is our "metered time." It is our "non-negotiable" boundary – our measure by which we make decisions. It insures operational integrity and provides a forum to seek and maintain common ground. Without it, our actions will be out of sync until our "moral compasses" are reset. Lifestyle "Metered Time" will keep you focused, and give you the basis on which to make wise decisions that are right for you.

Our personal and professional "metered time" transcends any company or team code of conduct. Written codes typically outline simple basics (respect for individual points of view, arriving on time, sticking to agreements, etc.) and are seldom taken seriously when the pressure of circumstances squeezes available resources. When the going gets tough, and the lines get fuzzy, we must have a clear strong understanding of what is nonnegotiable.

In our workshops, we ask everyone to close their eyes, then point in the direction of North. Then everyone opens their eyes, and realizes they are all pointing in different directions. It gets a great laugh. We then ask how we could be certain about which way was true north. The answer, of course, is to use a compass. In our lives, we also need to be certain about our "True North" – that internal compass that keeps us in line with our ethical beliefs and values. Members within our partnerships may express themselves in different ways, but the "Metered Timing" must serve as ethical guardrails to keep everyone moving in the same direction.

TIP FROM YOUR COACHES: Take time to clarify for yourself what your non-negotiables are. Then, stick to them.

In a good partnership, every step has its own feel...its own DNA. When he leads, she recognizes the feel for life.

The key is a sensitivity to your partner. You won't get anywhere without each other; it is a waste of time and energy to argue.

(Peter Billett, Fellow and Examiner of the Imperial Society of Teachers of Dancing; 9&10 Dance Champions, London; Finalist, USBC; United Kingdom Finalist, Ten Dance Championship; Imperial Trophy Winner, London)

DANCE WISDOM
(Ask yourself: How do these quotes relate to my business and my life?)

Slippery stages were the terror of my life.
(Fred Astaire, dance legend)

The psychological aspect of injury prevention is as important to the dancer as is proper conditioning and nutrition. Dancers, like other people, have varying personalities and react to stress in unique ways.
(Daniel Arnheim)

Flamenco is a living art form…its hybrid nature continues to be influenced by many other dance forms and…brings closely related cultures together. It's vigorous rhythmic dancing often inspires the audience to (applaud), stamp their feet and call out jaleos.
(Ilisa Rosal, Miami's first lady of Flamenco
& director of the Performing Arts Network)

A painting can be finished, but a dance can never be finished at rehearsal. Dance is a creation that needs the audience to be there, and only then can there be the whole creation. (Kei Takei)

MASTER OF MIME

DanceSport competitions are filled with triumphs and tragedies, phenomenal performances and political statements, glitz and glitter. The material rewards are few, and for the most part, insignificant. The true rewards are reflected in the winks of the judges and thunderous applause of the audience. Winning is held in perspective, because the joy felt by competitors lies in the dance performance itself. Consummate technical skills are expected from both amateur and professional, but it is the facial expressions and gestures that add the essential emotional component to a flawless technical performance. So "selling the movement" involves both the physical and emotional skills of the dancer.

A growing number of DanceSport competitors are using mime techniques to communicate both the mood and the emotional "translation" of the dance. Without the animating qualities of the face, movement and gestures can often seem contrived and mechanical. Hand movements must be intentional and relevant to both the motion and the "line" which characterize the classical "look" associated with ballroom choreography. Mime teaches competitors arm and hand coordination, concentration, space shifting and improvisation.

Hand, arm and facial expressions are not the focus of dance competitions; however, the movements must appear as natural extensions of the performance. They should not detract from a perfect line or sabotage the classical ballroom "look." They are part of the total package and function to sell each movement.

MASTER OF MIME
In Business And In Life

Actions speak louder than words. Successful people are those who can transcend technical competency, and integrate their entire body, mind and soul into their communications with others. In order to sell ideas and generate enthusiasm, you must become a master of mime – adding body language and facial expressions to support your message. We are always telegraphing information through our body language and facial expressions. To be truly powerful, we need to orchestrate the messages we are sending.

Like the mime who "manufactures" an imaginary wall or tugs convincingly at an invisible rope, we can use the skills of muscle and emotion to send messages to others. Control becomes critical, because we can give away our doubts and negative attitudes by our body language, too.

Mime skills also serve as a powerful tool for problem solving. Too often, we let words interfere with solutions; we get entangled in excuses, finger-pointing and pessimism. For mime-oriented people the space between problem and solution is considered illusionary. It exists only in the mind of the problem-solver. People schooled in mime pride themselves in turning hypothetical questions into highfalutin answers. They know how to create bridges to cross over problems and stairs to ascend to new heights.

TIP FROM YOUR COACHES: Practice the art of communicating emotions and ideas without using words. Create stories which have to be told strictly by mime. Then discuss what was really communicated. Try using mime to "talk" through a shared problem.

MAMBO MOOMBA

Originally forbidden fruit, the Mambo is named after voodoo priests who are believed to have been able to send devotees into wild, hypnotic dances. Of Cuban origin, the Mambo is a mixture of Afro-Caribbean and Latin America cultures. During its early years the famous American writer, Ernest Hemingway, spent so much drinking time in the bodegas (bars) of Havana that a Mambo move called El Mogito was named after him.

The Mambo is a dance of laid-back, joyful fun. Mambo-ing is a lyrical attempt to set the worries and stresses of the world aside for a while. It is a joyful "chilling-out" that brings laughter and lightness to the rigors of the day.

Moomba is an ancient Australian Aborigine term that, loosely translated, means "let's get together and have some fun!" Combining Mambo with Moomba captures the essence of finding hypnotic joy in ordinary things. It is a letting go of the sorcery of workaholism.

Dancers wise enough to send themselves into occasional wild, hypnotic dances of joy during rigorous workouts find practices a bit less burdensome. These Mambo Moomba experiences become emotional guardrails that keep dancers from becoming grim-faced workaholics.

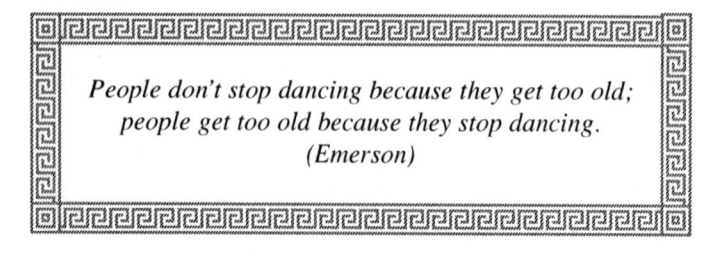

---

*People don't stop dancing because they get too old;
people get too old because they stop dancing.
(Emerson)*

MAMBO MOOMBA
In Business And In Life

People who become ashen-faced robots marching to the mechanical beat of the proverbial bottom line at work or the routineness of home life need a little bit of Mambo Moomba in their lives. Taunted by the demands of an increasingly hostile 21st Century, people are finding themselves stupefied by the crushing weight of work and home responsibilities. Down-sizings, cannibalistic mergers, mass lay-offs, family illnesses, divorces and natural disasters are disquieting reminders that anything can happen to anyone at any time.

At work, we are being asked to solve mammoth organizational problems as well as meet team performance objectives. We are being asked to operate in permanent "white water." At home the pressures are just as real. Lifestyle Moomba can be an emotional lifeboat on the fast moving currents of today's uncertainty. It gives us a chance to stop and catch our breaths – and wits – before we cruise toward the next crisis.

Lifestyle Moomba is our way of saying: Time-out. We're paying much too high of an emotional price for the work we're doing. Let's chill out for a while so we don't get seduced by the sorcery of workaholism, have-it-all-ism and know-it-all-ism.

TIP FROM YOUR COACHES: Use the Mambo Moomba when you feel life is too intense. Give yourself permission to call for a Lifestyle Moomba! Create a list of things you can do for fun – post it – and consult it often!

MOJO

The form of mysterious body wisdom that lets us know subconsciously what is going on with our big toe, gauges the limit of a hamstring stretch, or figures the extra couple of centimeters it takes for a perfect CBM (contrary body movement) is called kinesthetic sense. Many dancers call it "mojo." Quite literally, mojo is magical power. All of us have this magical internal ability to know what movement feels like kinesthetically, but few of us test our full range of motion the way dancers do.

Social ballroom dancers settle for basic-to-intermediate movements, while competitive DanceSport dancers explore the full range of movement available to them, depending on their level of athletic ability and experience.

Most social dancing is not about dance, per se, but about exploring interpersonal relationships and meeting new people. Advanced dance patterns are unnecessary. Competitive dancers, on the other hand (or is that foot?) must explore the possibilities of motion and extend the range of motion to produce award-winning choreography for open routines. The more in-tune they are with their "mojo," the more creative and effective they can be as dancers and performers. They trust their mojo to help them know instinctively how much risk to take and how far to stretch without causing permanent damage.

> *Part of his gift is that he is not just a world famous lindy hopper, he's an all around dancer, teaches jazz companies and is an accomplished social ballroom dancer, African dancer, and hip hop dancer—he's what they call a triple threat. (Louise Thwaite, Feather Award in Lindy Hop nominee commenting about Steven Mitchell, legendary lindy hopper)*

MOJO
In Business And In Life

When you don't tap into your "mojo", you are practicing the art of living and working by stumbling around. Lifestyle mojo is purposeful, decisive movement toward defined goals. It includes pushing the envelope – using all of our talents, resources and will power to achieve something we value. At work it means exploring all possibilities, honoring diversity, putting teamwork above individual agendas, seeking cross-functional alliances, and staying aware of lifestyle issues that affect team performance. At home it means treating family members as friends, not rivals; and taking the time to show everyone the respect and consideration they deserve.

When we tap into our kinesthetic sense, we know instinctively how far to push ourselves and others. We overcome internal fears and seek guidance, appreciating the fact that failing to ask for input from others may leave proverbial stones unturned, rendering solutions inaccessible.

Our mojo helps us grasp the value of self-care as a critical part of our regimen. For example, chronically bad eating habits affect lifestyle mojo if over-indulgences cause us to miss work or limit what we can achieve. Infighting and distrust wound our morale and cause us to move lethargically and disinterestedly. Without mojo, our movements become arthritic. If we slow down too much, emotional rigor mortis sets in. Simply put, lifestyle mojo is activity with accomplishment.

TIP FROM YOUR COACHES: Get in touch with lifestyle mojo by paying more attention to your intuition. Strengthen your intuition by responding to spontaneous urges. Assess the results, and reward yourself for listening to the instinctive, intuitive you.

NEGATIVE SPACE

Shaping is one of the most compelling and enduring visual components of ballroom dancing. It is one of the things that both the judges' eyes and audience's admiring gazes retain long after the competition is over. Shaping is the aesthetic sculptural design (imprint) of the couple's bodies, gestures and costumes.

The space competitive couples have to work *on* is the dance floor. The space the couple has to work *with* is a different matter. Experienced couples know how to surround themselves with negative space. Negative space is a visual arts term for the area surrounding an object which helps accent the object instead of diminishing or hiding it. The object is the "figure" and the area around it is referred to as "ground." For example, the shape of a tree in a meadow is defined by the space around it (the sky) and the negative spaces between the leaves and branches. What makes a single tree so difficult to see in a forest is the lack of surrounding (defining) negative space. Included in a dance couple's negative space are their competitors, photographers, and people moving about the ballroom.

The best competitive dancers move to the open areas of the dance floor to creative negative space between themselves and the rest of the couples. This tactic allows judges to see the couple's best choreography, undiminished and unclouded by another competitor's outstretched hand or flashy costume. Inexperienced couples misuse negative space by dancing too close to the judges, obstructing the adjudicators' view of the other dancers. This territorial intrusion generally backfires, because judges resent pushy performers who want to call blatant attention to themselves. Experienced couples use the negative space to differentiate themselves from hungry competitors.

NEGATIVE SPACE
In Business And In Life

People recognized for their ability to solve particularly knotty problems use the concept of negative space. Chaotic work and home environments are ground zero for most people. The more we identify ourselves with chaotic environments by remaining part of them, the less negative space we have at our disposal. Teams mired in organizational difficulties remain part of the problem, not the solution. Family members who stay immersed in family squabbles limit their ability to be objective.

Negative lifestyle space is the physical, emotional, psychological and technological space we place between ourselves (figure) and the nagging issues at hand (ground). People who are good at surrounding themselves with negative space distance themselves from the confusion and stress of thorny problems and make negative space the dominant theme of decision-making and problem-solving.

Highly effective teams may work in chaotic environments, but they work with negative space to produce positive results. Highly successful families are able to separate context and expediency from cherished family values and make good decisions.

TIP FROM YOUR COACHES: Create negative space by changing the physical context of a situation. For example, conduct team meetings away from the normal work environment. Be on the lookout for novel sites that allow team members to breathe, talk, problem-solve, laugh and create – without the jarring disruptions of a chaotic workplace. Take the family on a weekend retreat that includes rest and relaxation, panel discussions on thorny issues, role plays and quiet time.

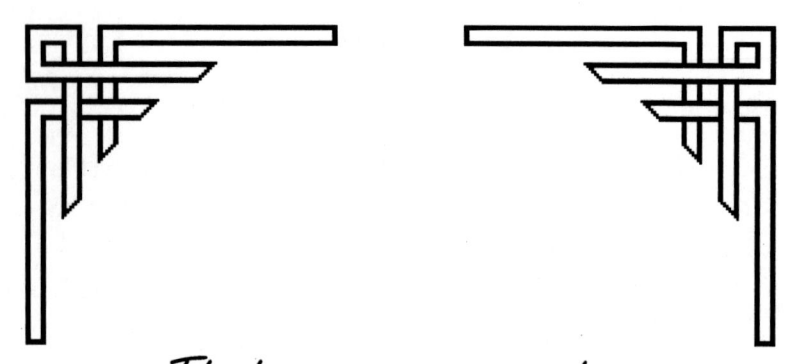

The best practices are those when you treat your partner with respect and courtesy...just as you want to be treated.

Most arguments are over trivial things and not worth time and energy we put in it.

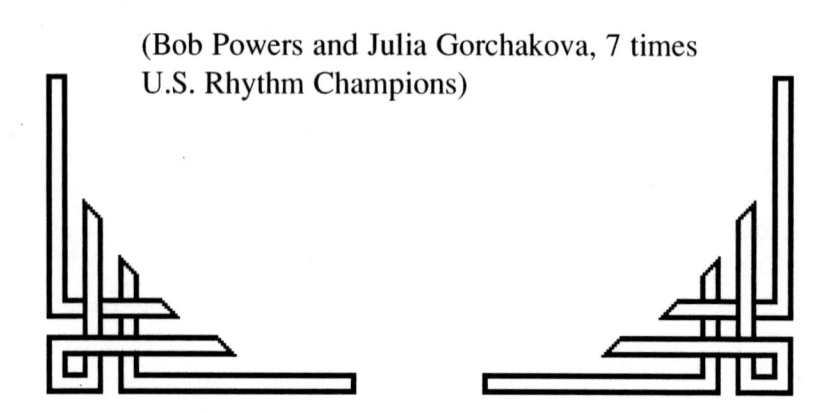

(Bob Powers and Julia Gorchakova, 7 times U.S. Rhythm Champions)

DANCE WISDOM
(Ask yourself: How do these quotes relate to my business and my life?)

Discipline is the key in dance and in life. Achieve a balance between the analytical and emotional sides.
(Ann Harding, DanceSport Judge, Coach, and Competitor)

I always felt an added excitement when performing to a live orchestra. It seemed to improve the quality of the dancing and encourage participation from the audience.
(Nadia Eftedal, Former Open British Latin Champion)

(American Smooth) is the most complex and comprehensive form of (ballroom) dancing...because...you need a good understanding of the International Standard, the same partnership skills in Latin, all the same floorcraft in the Standard, and all of the other theatrical abilities of theater, ballet, jazz dancing, Irish step dancing, clogging and (then you combine all of that) into one style.
(Michelle Officer, American Smooth Ballroom National Champion)

I look for kinetic energy flying off the ends of the performer's fingers.
(Debra Brown, choreographer for Cirque du Soleil)

PARQUET PIETY

Each day a dancer doesn't dance causes small bits of the dancer's talent to erode. Like a rotting floor, little-by-little, the dancer ceases to exist. Peerless mastery comes from immersion, not neglect. The study and practice of any art form, from ballroom dancing and music to painting and sculpting, must be pursued for its own sake, for the highly private and personal pleasure it brings, and for the multitude of ways it shapes character and encourages others. It is disciplined discipleship. Like any art form, ballroom dancing becomes a personal metaphor for soul growth. Daily communion with an art form elevates performance because devotion to anything deepens the relationship between the faithful and the object of that devotion. The best dancers are dutiful to their craft, and piety is not too strong a word. The true ballroom dance enthusiast practices religiously every day.

Competitive ballroom dancing is about partnership, personality and piety. It is the language of sophisticated closeness, high fashion, grace and discipline. It is partnership dancing from the inside out. Ballroom dancing at its best is the transformation of feelings into the physics of tandem body movement. It takes complete immersion to unite two believers into one unit of graceful choreography. And when the immersion is complete, the synergy is breathtaking.

It takes years of "parquet-time" to excel at ballroom dancing. Thinking about it won't suffice. Talking about ballroom techniques won't do it. Dreaming about partnership dancing won't cut it. Couples have to "cut" the floor for a long time before they dance like one unit. And so, parquet time literally means parquet piety.

PARQUET PIETY
In Business And In Life

People differ not only in their *ability* to do but also in their *willingness* to do. Successful people have more will power than won't power. Their willingness to work toward a common goal unites their efforts and turns individual responsibilities into mutual accountabilities. High end commitment is disciplined discipleship. And like any true believer, conscientious people devote themselves to getting a job done, and getting it done right.

Parquet piety in business and in life is commitment to the process. It means putting in the time to create the partnerships. In a very real sense, work for lifestyle conscious people is a vocation, a calling. To do "bad" work is to cause injury to the soul of the work, the spirit of the team and the integrity of the family. Working soulfully and dutifully brings a certain amount of piety to each day's labor.

Lifestyle piety means spending time together to become one. Reading about teamwork or family solidarity won't cut it; watching videos or listening to motivational speakers won't create it; wishful thinking or management mandates will not produce it. Unity comes only from religiously working through "stuff" as a unit. People living at the speed of reverential life know that piety is not too strong a word.

TIP FROM YOUR COACHES: Make a personal commitment to invest the time necessary to build a strong relationship. You can't learn how to have a great partnership from reading books any more than you can learn dancing from a book. You have to get out on the floor and do it!

THE PASO DOBLE

One of the most electrifying and dramatic dances in the world of ballroom dancing is the Paso Doble. When it comes to performance, the degree of technical expertise, athleticism, stamina and dramatics required to perform the Paso keeps many dancers at a respectful distance. Generally danced to variations of España Cani (the Spanish Gypsy Dance), the Paso features the gentleman in the role of a matador and the lady as his cape in the drama of the traditional Spanish bull-fight.

The mood of the dance is broad-shouldered, full-chested masculinity on the part of the gentleman. He must strut and prance his way across the parquet floor at his macho best. The woman, who is his shadow as the cape, must project an attitude of haughtiness, contemptuousness, and aloofness. Each half of the partnership must complement the other's powerful performance in order to "sell" the Paso.

Dancers can learn the technique, styling and school figures of the Paso Doble, but unless they are willing to "play the part" and put their whole being into the characterization, they cannot "sell" the emotional components of Paso.

It's not the same to talk of bulls as to be in the bullring. (Spanish Proverb)

THE PASO DOBLE
In Business And In Life

In today's ambush-prone 21st Century, people who hide behind aging technologies, antiquated beliefs or stagnant attitudes will be hard-pressed to defend and amend themselves. Businesses who cannot stomach repeated attacks by hungry, customer-obsessed competitors or recover from token support from management will be brought to their collective knees. People who have been around family sorry-go-rounds a few times know that chaotic environments can rough up a family and strain relationships when bullish attempts to dominate people occur.

The mood of lifestyle Paso has to be one of assertiveness and decisiveness whenever people are faced with hostile business or family environments. Survival often means asking for forgiveness instead of approval. Aggressive movement toward defined goals is a defining characteristic of lifestyle Paso. Lifestyle Paso requires audacity and persistence to prevent oneself from being "gored" by the status quo or bullish people.

Many people go through the motions of team work, but they are not able to hide their brutish individuality. Success demands that everyone becomes fully committed to achieving agreed-upon goals. The involvement has to be real, or people will discover that "bullishness" has to be controlled, channeled and finessed in family, social and business arenas.

TIP FROM YOUR COACHES: Build lifestyle Paso by assessing everyone's commitment. Create an august mood by playing The Spanish Gypsy Dance and having everyone emulate the antics of a world-renowned Matador who is able to handle bullish problems.

PIVOTS

One of the most enjoyable ballroom movements to watch is the Pivot. As a couple spins around each other, while moving down the floor, spectators are captivated by the magic of the seemingly effortless floating motion. In reality, pivots are advanced moves in any ballroom dance syllabus. Keeping the proper body alignment is paramount. Heads must be slightly slanted away from the other partner, hips and thighs tightly connected, frame maintained at all points through the pivot and faces postured toward the momentum of the turn. Add to the above requirements the importance of rotating the supporting foot, getting out of the "driving" partner's rotational initiative and progressing along the line of dance. Trust us – it isn't easy!

Pivots take eye-hand coordination, balance, control, patience and partnership. The centrifugal force generated by coordinated energies spins the couple across the floor like a top. The more accelerated the spin, the tighter the hip and thigh connection must be maintained. Like a top, tapering from its wideness to a point, the couple must keep their shoulders, heads and arms apart while maintaining pelvic contact. Otherwise the spin will wobble to and fro, disrupt the centrifugal force and disintegrate the pivot, sending the couple out-of-control.

When done correctly, pivots use the relationship between centrifugal force, change-of-direction, acceleration and de-acceleration to produce a choreographed turn. Pivotal movements – seemingly out-of-control – are, in reality, an orchestrated series of exquisitely-timed tandem maneuvers by a talented dance couple who fully understand and execute the natural laws involving two dancers in motion.

PIVOTS
In Business And In Life

Have you ever noticed how some people are devastated from the rough experiences in life, while others seem to magically glide through them, coming out way ahead? Lifestyle pivots can help us deal with the about-faces or turning points in our lives. They are the essence of changes in direction which stem from alterations to our course, throwing us off our trajectories. When life seems to throw us out of control, lifestyle pivots can bring us back in control.

Lifestyle pivots are turn-on-a-dime tactics that help us roll with the punches, much like ballroom dancers employ to "dodge" another couple on crowded dance floors. However, when a couple loses focus of center, their pivots go out of control and they must immediately stop or find themselves careening crazily down the floor. So it is in life. When you find yourself out of control, chances are you have lost your focus. The more you try to compensate, the more out of control things become. The best tactic is to come to a complete stop, refocus, and begin again.

Having the tools to stay centered and focused while spinning through a life event make the difference between failure and success. What may look like a risky spin is, in reality, an orchestrated, well-rehearsed pivot, moving us quickly to a whole new level of expertise.

TIP FROM YOUR COACHES: For pivots to succeed, they must be well rehearsed. Anticipate potential problems you may encounter and then strategize your lifestyle pivots. Include techniques to stay focused and centered, such as deep breathing, meditation and relaxation.

PROMENADE

Promenades are not as simple as they appear. When done correctly, they are what is known in the dance business as "compromise" steps. Essentially each member of the couple moves forward, toward and against his/her partner. The lady moves forward toward diagonal center and the gentleman moves forward toward diagonal wall. This slight opposing action by both members of the couple actually sends the couple into promenade as their energies meet in the middle of the movement and force the couple into a controlled tangential movement.

Expertly executed promenades use the equal and opposite energies of the couple to parade or promenade across the floor. Although the couple remains in a closed body position (standard body contact at the hips and thighs) the progression is forward along the line of dance with both the gentleman and lady facing in the direction of travel.

Promenades are "touring" moves, which suggest brief excursions or pleasure trips as couples "reach consensus" and prance their stuff across the dance floor.

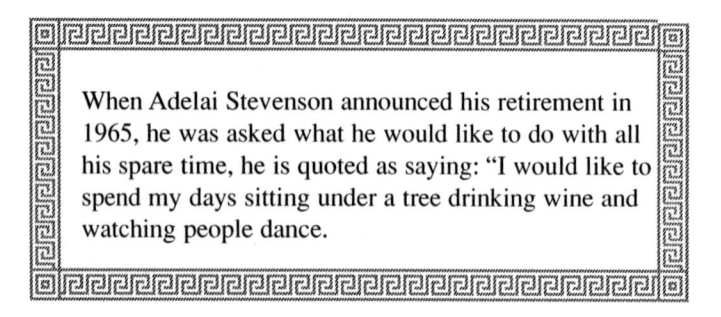

When Adelai Stevenson announced his retirement in 1965, he was asked what he would like to do with all his spare time, he is quoted as saying: "I would like to spend my days sitting under a tree drinking wine and watching people dance.

PROMENADE –
In Business And In Life

Any attempt to reach mutually acceptable solutions to nagging problems calls for a lifestyle promenade. Lifestyle promenades involve seeking expedient, middle-ground agreements to engineer compromise. Lifestyle promenades work best when people want the same thing but disagree on how to get there. Expertly executed lifestyle promenades occur when opponents "split the difference" between opposing viewpoints and move in the same direction.

Lifestyle promenades differ from the classic types of conflict resolution strategies because they amalgamate the positive aspects of several types of conflict management styles. Lifestyle promenades use aspects of competing, accommodating, collaborating and compromising styles to make lifestyle promenade work. Lifestyle promenades borrow the defensive attitude from competing; hospitality from the accommodating style; cooperation and synergy from the collaborating style; and mutual concessions from the compromising style. The impetus of the amalgamation is to move people toward defined goals and objectives without compromising the group's principles.

In essence, when partners in business or in life are faced with differing viewpoints, they can mimic the ballroom promenade by staying centered and focused on the same goals and values.

TIP FROM YOUR COACHES: When faced with conflict, move to a lifestyle promenade by insuring that everyone is facing the same direction (the desired goal). Allow everyone to express concerns, then look for areas of agreement first. Ask what it will take to reach a consensus.

I keep this quote hanging at my kitchen desk:

*Speak kind words . . .
Hear kind echoes!*

(Vivienne Ramsey, 5 times World Exhibition Champion; 4 times (Blackpool) British Exhibition Champion; 3 times U.S. Exhibition champion; 2 times Triple Crown Champion; former soloist with Hamburg Ballet, Germany; wife and mother of two!)

... in business and in life

DANCE WISDOM
(Ask yourself: How do these quotes relate to my business and my life?)

Don't hold grudges! While you're holding grudges, they're out dancing!
(Buddy Hackett)

If your aim is to become a famous dancer... you're working for a noun and nouns never last as long as verbs. So make certain that dancing is what you love to do and... dance as well as you can.
(Paul Draper, legendary dancer in tap, jazz, classical music and ballet)

If there were only one required subject at Harvard, I would make it dancing.

(Charles W. Eliot, former President Harvard University)

Somantics is about how you can reorganize neuromuscular patterns so the execution of dance technique produces what you hope it's going to produce, which is a wide range of movement qualities for the dancer.
(Martha Myers, Dean of the American Dance Festival)

QUICKSTEPPING

The Quickstep owes its existence to a pre-World War I American comedian named Harry Fox who invented the Foxtrot in 1915. The Foxtrot evolved into the Quick Foxtrot around 1920 and competed with the Charleston by 1925 as the most popular dance in the roaring twenties. The two dances were combined in the late twenties, forming a dance called the Quickstep. At its most competitive, the Quickstep is an international dance which features a combination of swing movements and elaborately syncopated hops, lock steps, cortés, chassés and turns danced at impressive speeds.

While the dance gives the appearance of joyful abandon and free-spirited moves, it is only an illusion. In reality, the quickstep requires extreme discipline, exquisite partnership, highly-developed technical expertise, and well-choreographed movements. Otherwise, dancers find themselves crashing into one another or unceremoniously being trampled under the feet of other competitors. We've seen it happen!

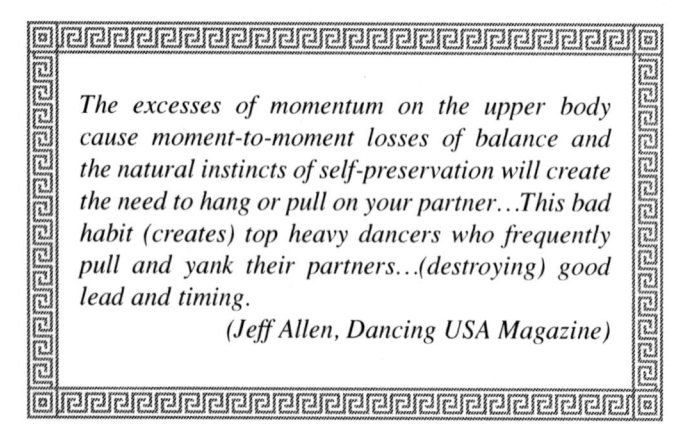

> *The excesses of momentum on the upper body cause moment-to-moment losses of balance and the natural instincts of self-preservation will create the need to hang or pull on your partner...This bad habit (creates) top heavy dancers who frequently pull and yank their partners...(destroying) good lead and timing.*
>
> *(Jeff Allen, Dancing USA Magazine)*

QUICKSTEPPING
In Business And In Life

"Done is better than perfect" is the philosophy which defines lifestyle quickstepping. Indecision or a desire for perfection interfere with team or family success. Too many of us suffer from paralysis by analysis. We choose to hide behind reams of information before we act. Unfortunately, we may never obtain (or even need) the information we seek, and the moment of absolute certainty we savor may never arrive.

Although it is important to demand the credentials of facts, we need to add a few quick intuitions and speedy hunches to our decision-making repertoire to turbo-charge our success. Quickstepping in business and in life can achieve far better results than slowly and methodically getting bogged down in details.

This does not mean that you should just forge ahead without thought or information. In order to successfully perform lifestyle quickstepping, you must have highly-developed technical and process skills, and strong relationships with others who can provide guidance and advice. Otherwise, you'll find yourself tripping over poor planning, reinventing wheels and sabotaging the doable with misplaced steps and poorly-timed changes in direction – all leaving you unceremoniously being trampled under the feet of other competitors.

TIP FROM YOUR COACHES: Constantly ask yourself two questions: "How can I move ahead more quickly?" and "How can I make this easier?" Then do it!

SWEAT SUITE

We like to refer to a dance studio's practice floor area as the "Sweat Suite". Salty pearls of sweat anoint a dancer's body during rigorous rehearsals and practices, making practices spiritual events and purifying rituals that unite body, mind and spirit. The fatigue felt from marathon work-outs is a cleansing fatigue and the aches and pains remind dancers that there are limits to human endurance.

Practice sweat is the perfect performance tonic because it means the dancer spent enough parquet time to perfect the required syllabus figures. It takes time to sweat. Sweating means a vigorous workout has taken place and vigorous workouts mean commitment to excellence. It doesn't matter how much a dancer knows about ballroom dancing. He/she must be willing to break a sweat on a regular basis to excel in the craft. Knowledge is one thing, but it is experience – floor time – that makes ballroom dance champions. Why? Because an ounce of joyful, disciplined dancing is worth a ton of theory.

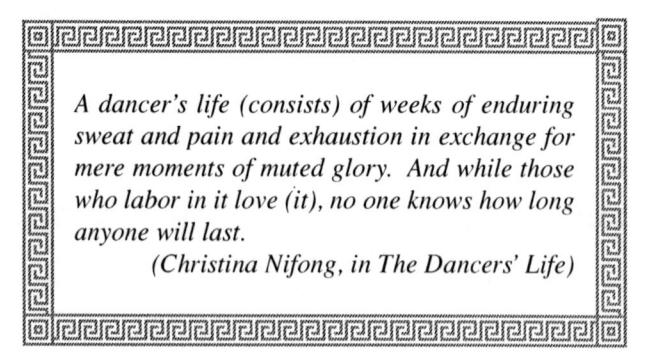

> *A dancer's life (consists) of weeks of enduring sweat and pain and exhaustion in exchange for mere moments of muted glory. And while those who labor in it love (it), no one knows how long anyone will last.*
> *(Christina Nifong, in The Dancers' Life)*

SWEAT SUITE
In Business And In Life

Lifestyle sweat is a metaphor for living at the speed of commitment. It means spending enough time with personal relationships, personal challenges, and personal fitness to "break a sweat." It's about immersion, commitment, and sense of duty – not forced cooperation and compliance. The reason businesses, as well as families, must commit themselves to virtues and values is that after all of the toils, troubles and trumpeting, tomorrows become todays, and our choices create our realities. Commitment and persistence have no colloquial, regional or partisan accents. Everyone in the family or on the team has to add his/her sweat to everyone else's sweat.

The more a team sweats (the higher the commitment) the less it becomes a work group joined by the mechanical squares, dots and lines drawn on organization charts. Families which sweat together generally stay together through "thick and thin." Team effort is concerted effort. Some efforts require more sweat than others, so don't be pedestrian in your efforts.

Commitment is present tense effort. It is not something you talk about, it's something you do.

TIP FROM YOUR COACHES: No matter how busy or geographically separated, it is critical that people who mean the most to each other spend quality time together. Arrange for periodic face-to-face meetings, off-site team sessions, family reunions and long week-ends to build commitment, closeness and kinship in your own personal "Sweat Suite."

RELEVÈ

Relevé is a dance move that requires the dancer to elevate the body through the full extension of the leg, by rising up onto the toes. It is important to note that the relevé cannot be performed properly if a dancer tries to execute it from straight legs. To be done properly, the relevé is preceded by a plié (knees bent outward with the back held straight). This serves as a preparation to give the body momentum as the dancer stretches into the relevé move.

DanceSport and theatre arts competitors perform these plié/relevé movements repeatedly during their rehearsals, almost ritual-like, because they know pliés and relevés build strength in the hips, legs and knees. By using the relevé as a practice tool, they are prepared to create the beautiful flow which characterizes ballroom dancing, particularly the rise and fall of the waltz and foxtrot. A well-executed relevé gives the appearance of defying gravity.

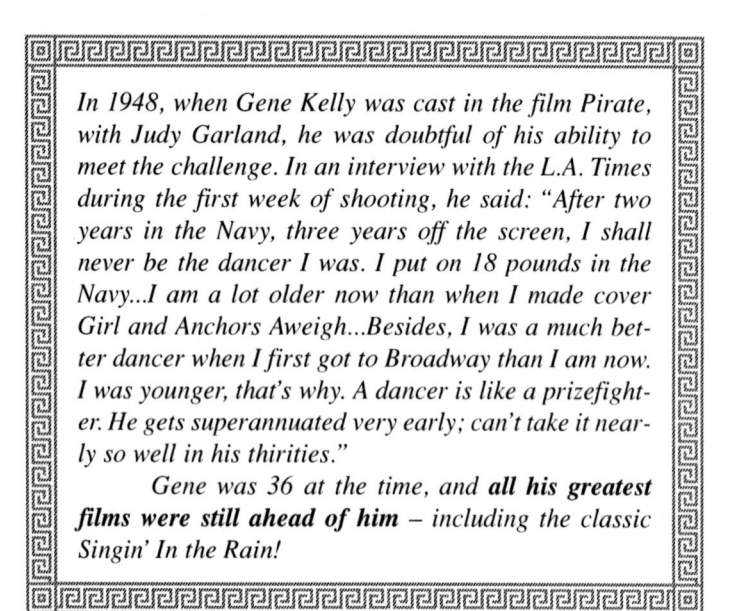

> In 1948, when Gene Kelly was cast in the film Pirate, with Judy Garland, he was doubtful of his ability to meet the challenge. In an interview with the L.A. Times during the first week of shooting, he said: "After two years in the Navy, three years off the screen, I shall never be the dancer I was. I put on 18 pounds in the Navy...I am a lot older now than when I made cover Girl and Anchors Aweigh...Besides, I was a much better dancer when I first got to Broadway than I am now. I was younger, that's why. A dancer is like a prizefighter. He gets superannuated very early; can't take it nearly so well in his thirities."
>
> Gene was 36 at the time, and **all his greatest films were still ahead of him** – including the classic Singin' In the Rain!

RELEVÈ
In Business And In Life

You must lift yourself above the gravity of circumstances and non-productive pull of any situation which affects your ability to live life to the fullest. When facing difficulties, you must relevé (rise) to the occasion to guarantee success. Sometimes our legs lock, and we lose our will to move through problems. Progress slows or stops. When that happens, the gravity of the situation makes it hard to relevé, bringing good intentions to a standstill.

Lifestyle relevé is confidence, willpower and high expectations of success. Will power and faith are related, and one usually reinforces the other. This constancy to purpose is what keeps our spirit and aspirations elevated. The greatest gains in our success are realized through our persistent efforts to relevé over obstacles and disappointments instead of stooping in defeat before them.

Another way to put it: When life gives you pliés, use them to create phenomenal relevés!

TIP FROM YOUR COACHES: Use the 5-10-15 Technique to relevé yourself above disappointment, depression or frustration. Set a timer for 5 minutes, and use this time to allow yourself to wallow in your negative feelings. When the alarm rings, reset it for 10 minutes, during which you must counter every negative thought or feeling with a positive one. When the alarm rings this time, reset it for 15 minutes. During this time, you must be completely positive, saying uplifting things, moving around the room, singing, and affirming success.

I always get students that make mistakes in their routines prior to going to the competition and up until the practice right before the competition. To ease their anxiety, I always say, "Remember there are no mistakes in dancing. If the man does something other than the routine it is a variation, if it is the lady, it is styling." That seems to ease the anxiety and they step out on the floor to try and do their best.

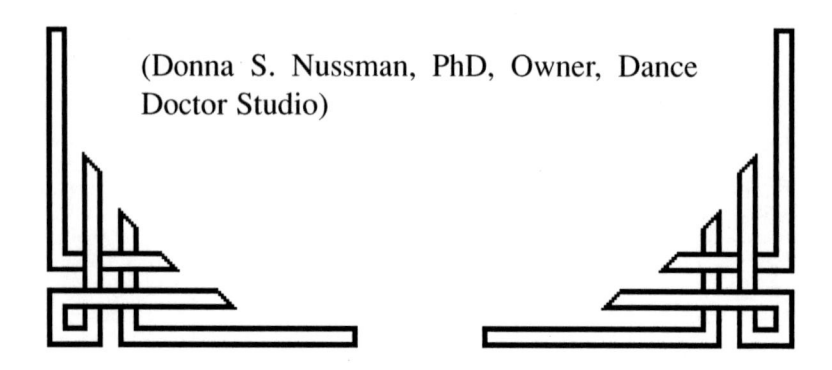

(Donna S. Nussman, PhD, Owner, Dance Doctor Studio)

DANCE WISDOM
(Ask yourself: How do these quotes relate to my business and my life?)

The key thing is to believe that the achievement of goals is not that important. It's the process of attempting to achieve the goals that should be primary.
(Fernando Bujones, American Ballet Theatre Star)

If dancers can rid themselves of their illusions of youthfulness, and if dance-goers are willing to admit that dancers can be human beings as well as gods or angels, then dance may at least...be an art for all ages.
(Jack Anderson, columnist)

Here's a conversation I frequently have with myself during casting: "Hm, that person doesn't have as much technique as I'd like but they're communicating such joy when they dance. I'm going to hire them anyway."
(Peggy Hickey, MTV award-winning choreographer)

Communication is what dancing is all about.
(Marge Champion, legendary ballroom dancer, actress, choreographer)

LET'S RUMBA

Unquestionably, Rumba is the dance of love. The dance itself broadcasts the strength, confidence and sexuality of the flirtatious male as the archetypal lover whose unbridled passion tempts his partner to lower her inhibitions and join him in the music of love and romance. Characteristically, however, women play roles of coyness, teasing and toying with their male partner by first luring him then rejecting his constant amorous advances.

The rhythm of Rumba is patient enticement. It is a sort of hot "smoldering" to represent romantic interest coated with coyness, as the passions of the dancers are slow and deliberate. Although conquest is the goal, its prerequisites are shared respect, mutual sensuality and controlled longing. Rumba is an intimate dance, but its rules are clear – mutual consent and legitimate affection are paramount to consummating the dance relationship.

When the rumba is performed by a talented dance team, the spectators can literally feel the heat flow through their own bodies. A rumba invites you in, making you part of the passion and drama, fluidity and movement of the dance.

If you watch carefully, you will notice that there is continual movement throughout the entire rumba. While the dancers will frequently hit a pose, there is always a movement of the arm, head or torso. This continual flow creates a vision of fluidity that is similar to a good movie. There is always something happening, but every movement contributes to the overall story being told.

LET'S RUMBA
In Business And In Life

The best performing teams and the highest achieving families realize that one of the keys to sustained accomplishment and competitive muscle is cultivating an innovation-rich environment. More and more, progressive, tuned-in businesses and families faithfully tempt the Muse out of her intuitive lair so she can reveal solutions to nagging problems. When you want to seduce the Muse, make your credo "Let's rumba!"

Creativity and innovation fuel a team's longevity and foster its capacity to create wealth. Teams who dance with the Muse also flirt with her. Her amorous winks (insights) and smiles (hunches) come readily once she knows the team wants to rumba.

Families can court the Muse, too. Creative and innovative families can triumph over conformity, health challenges, obnoxious personalities, work demands and any other family challenge. All they have to do is take the Muse home from work and dance the night away. The same innovation techniques that work in business work at home. Lifestyle rumba is the dance of the love of life. Seeing life's hardships as part of the dance helps families see the relationship between honest effort, hardship, joy, peace and faith. All of our life's experiences are steps in the dance of life. So if you want to "rumba" with life, tempt the Muse more often so you can create the kind of lifestyle you want.

TIP FROM YOUR COACHES: Use the phrase "Let's Rumba!" as a cue to generate creativity and action, drawing everyone in the partnership into the action.

SALSA

Originally Venezuelan, the Salsa has Cuban, Puerto Rican, Haitian and Afro-Caribbean roots. In 1928 Ignzcio Piñeiro used the phrase "Echale Salsita" to describe his music. The phrase was simplified to Salsa which means "spice it up." And the name has stuck. Salsa, as a dance, mirrors musically a diversity of dozens of other dance styles and rhythms. Some moves are taken from traditional dances, others are adapted from jazz, modern dance and other Latin variations. Some moves were and are invented to express the relaxed style of the Salsa.

Turns and repetitive moves are key features of the Salsa and illustrate the repetitious musicality of the dance. The best Salseros generate turns during preceding movements to "ease" into the next turn. The value of Salsa as an art form is the way it morphs the old with the new. It is a cumulative art form. It is constantly evolving, as a "dance in flux" to fuse the traditional with the transitional.

"Spicing it up" can create problems. In the movie Top Hat, for the dance number Dancing Cheek to Cheek, Ginger Rogers wore an unusual dress created of feathers. During the rehearsal, the feathers began to fly – literally! The shots were obscured by the fluffy blizzard, and feathers invaded Fred Astaire's nose, eyes and mouth! During the night before the final filming, all the extra feathers were collected, and a costume crew pulled an "all-nighter" to stitch each feather securely in place. Even so, if you look closely, you'll see a few feathers flying during the scene.

Fred and choreographer Hermes Pan actually composed a parody of the song, beginning with the words: *Feathers, I hate feathers . . .*

SALSA
In Business And In Life

Lifestyle salsa means to spice up the tired old with the revitalizing new. The first rule of salsa is: you have to improve something in both your work and family environments that benefits everyone. It can be something as simple as replacing old furniture and equipment or a bit more eloquent like stream-lining corporate communications or visiting a long-lost relative. Adding copious amounts of seasoning (creativity, innovation, respect, thoughtfulness, compassion, open communications, authenticity, etc.) to old recipes (bureaucratic rigor mortis, status-quo woes, the-way-we've-always-done-things mentality, etc.)brings zest and vitality to relationships at work and at home.

The second rule of salsa is: life is an experiment sweetened by risks. Risk-averse people are afraid to experiment. Consequently, they fail to see the possibilities associated with adding a pinch of innovation here, a tad of trust there, a slice of insight over there, and so on. Businesses and families who are "spice" aversive usually fail to accomplish anything of value. The real danger businesses and families face in the new millennium is not the amount of educated risks they take, but the number of staid precautions they settle for in what they think are safe environments.

TIP FROM YOUR COACHES: Use the *Salsa Technique* to add spice to your life: Once a month do something you have never done before. It can be simple (try a new food; have a team meeting in a different room) or major (sky dive; ask for a meeting with the president of the company; adopt a new hobby). The key is to constantly add new experiences to your life and your partnerships.

SELL THE SIZZLE

If the American Smooth (Waltz, Tango, Foxtrot and Viennese Waltz) and International Standard (adds quickstep to the traditional four in American Standard) echo the protocols and formalities of royal courts and upper-class ballrooms, the American Rhythm and Latin dances reflect the fast-lane life of the barrios of Havana, the vias of Rio De Janero, the nightclubs of Harlem, and the bullfight arenas of Madrid.

In the hot and flashy Latin dances, courtship remains the language of unbridled emotion, but the message is often flirtation, passion, lust and eroticism. Accelerating legs, hips and pelvis ignite the dance floor. The non-stop motion sizzles like electricity through heaving chests, contouring shoulders, expressive faces, and precise arm and hand movements as it flashes its scintillating energy from manicured fingertips like lightning.

The flashy costumes of Latin and Rhythm dancers underwrite their passion for exhibitionism and free expression. Men choose blousy satin and knit shirts, unbuttoned to reveal rippling pectorals and fine jewelry. Their trousers (almost always black) flatten the stomach, sculpt the buttocks and accent musculared legs.

Women model costumes that embody sensuality and chic-ness. The mesh, knit and exotic styling of the colorful material accents the superb physiques of their tanned bodies and carries sensuality to the heights of the imagination. The effect is intentionally seductive and disarming.

But costumes alone are only the sizzle. The mood is mesmerized respect for two performers who are putting their body, mind and soul into highly-disciplined, but thoroughly entertaining performances. They sell the sizzle with talent.

SELL THE SIZZLE
In Business And In Life

Within any partnership, skills and expertise alone won't cut it. To be truly successful, you have to create some kind of "sizzle." This is what makes individuals stand out, move to the top and tower a head above the rest.

To be truly effective, of course, people must offer solutions and benefits, not merely bells and whistles. They treat customers, colleagues, relatives and friends as appreciating assets. They know that people buy "sizzle," but the product, service or relationship had better live up to the sizzle. An item's sizzle value is based on its quality and relevance because people trust results more than promises or good intentions.

Lifestyle Sizzle is a coordinated and impassioned effort to accentuate the unique qualities a person has to offer. When you practice Lifestyle Sizzle, you reach into your true self, and pull out the best you have to offer. You bring to any partnership that sparkle, that creativity, that originality that magnetizes others to you.

But it must go deeper than the sizzle alone. There are lots of people who project sizzle, but if it isn't supported by values, skill and ethical credibility, the sizzle will fizzle and the partnership will fail. The ones that can consistently "sell the sizzle" and build long-lasting relationships are the ones who provide the value they promise.

TIP FROM YOUR COACHES: Within each partnership, ask these questions: What makes us unique and different? What is our "sizzle?" Are we living up to what we project and promise?

SITSTILLA

Okay – we admit it! We made this word up! But it is an interesting concept that describes a phenomenon in ballroom dancing that seems to have no other word. It is that ability to settle into the knees and pause, in order to move ahead to the next beat of music.

Because ballroom dancing involves both feet and bodies in motion, dancers must concern themselves with overcoming inertia to move smoothly from one static position to another. When a dance movement begins, the competitors' bodies move through space. There must be shifts in weight in the direction of travel in order to overcome the inertia of bodies at rest. Stepping forward, for example, requires a shift in weight forward and then a receiving of the weight transfer to the new base of support—the trailing foot. The timing of the weight shift and the placement of the trailing foot is variable depending on the particular dance.

In the Foxtrot, which is danced to 4/4 time, the initial movement by the dancers is to lower on beat one and begin the forward motion on beat two. Beats three and four are steps, but the couple must in flight to lower again on the first beat of the next sequence of beats. It is that hesitation (settling) on the first beat that defines the Foxtrot and distinguishes it from its cousin the Waltz.

This partnership with inertia produces the rhythmic and stylistic movements associated with ballroom dancing. Knowing when to sitstilla (settle) into the movement, spin out of a turn, change direction, and control momentum are skills developed through countless hours of experience. Overcoming inertia stylishly is the hallmark of world-class DanceSport couples. It gives them liquid grace and picturesque movement.

SITSTILLA
In Business And In Life

Sometimes people need to "sitstilla" for a while. One of the strategies used to revitalize, enliven and enlighten people is the retreat. If handled effectively these "sitstilla" events galvanize people who take time-out from the rigors of work. We call a sitstilla events a "retreat forward":
- *retreat (a going back, withdrawal to a safe place, a place for contemplation);*
- *forward (to send ahead, of or for the future)*

As such, these events can be productivity preserves, recuperative pauses and temporary recesses to revitalize a business's or a family's spirit. Once resuscitated, participants can step back into the routineness of current responsibilities without further hesitation.

If people "sitstilla" long enough, they may find answers to important life issues like: defining core values and one's purpose, improving important relationships, settling conflicts, clarifying commitments, boosting morale, managing change, building camaraderie, crystallizing goals, managing conflict, and so on. But you must be careful not to stay in the sitstilla too long, or you'll miss the next beat of music and create a distorted dance movement.

TIP FROM YOUR COACHES: Schedule a Sitstilla Retreat Forward event for your team, family or partnership. Have very specific goals or outcomes for the event, then structure the time away so you are all revitalized and recharged, ready to move back into "real life" with liquid grace and picturesque movement.

Magic happens when the feminine aligns with the masculine. The man gives of his strength and the woman gives of her sensitivity to create a new union. Powerful emotions are created with the union of sensuality and beautiful bodies moving in harmony that far exceed any heights that can be attained as an individual.

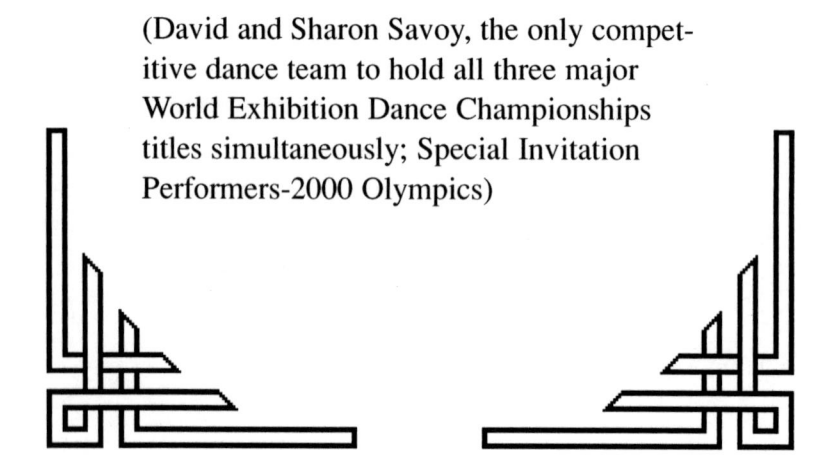

(David and Sharon Savoy, the only competitive dance team to hold all three major World Exhibition Dance Championships titles simultaneously; Special Invitation Performers-2000 Olympics)

DANCE WISDOM
(Ask yourself: How do these quotes relate to my business and my life?)

To (those) who turn away from dance, I have but one question: Is (it) a choice between two loves, or is it a choice between a love and what is "practical," or "sensible," or "safe?" To choose a probably successful (career) for which you have neither the hunger nor passion but only the press of rationalized necessity is to fail as you begin. To succeed at what you do not love is to fail from the go.
(Daniel Nagrin, legendary dancer, Professor Emeritus, Arizona State University)

I like dancers who want to explore with me and share something new where we may fail or succeed, but who will go out on a limb with me emotionally. If we fail, we weep...if we succeed, we sing... but eitherway we are together.
(Gillian Lynne, award-winning choreographer of Phantom of the Opera and Cats)

There are some dancers I (refuse) to work with. Dancers of this cut are usually late (for auditions); they don't warm up thoroughly, are unfocused...use cell phones on breaks to book another gig...ask to leave early for another audition...or job. This illustrates total disrespect for the project, their fellow dancers, me and ultimately themselves.
(Vincent Patterson, choreographer of the Birdcage and Evita)

One must have chaos in oneself to be a dancing star.
(Nietzche, philosopher)

THE SOCIAL CONTRACT

In the art of ballroom dancing, the most ancient of languages finds its expression in the new millennium: body language. The depth and beauty of human relationships are enshrined in dance. A physical dialogue takes place. Sometimes it's scintillating, romantic, exotic. Other times disciplined, elegant and subdued. But ballroom dancing has a special dimension that makes it different than all other forms of dance. It has a social aspect to it, and it is this quality that weds ballroom dancing to the masses.

Ballet, modern dance, stage duets, acrobatic-etudes, cabarets, aerobic performances and tap are all complicated dance forms which distance performers' abilities from the abilities of the general public. Although competitive ballroom dancing features arabesque, attitudes, fouettees, grand jetes, splits, dévelopés and even battements, its finer elements are "public friendly." Social dancers can perform these moves with coaching and a little practice.

The social contract involved in dancing socially makes ballroom dancing universal. Music, human-touch, mutual respect and love for dancing are the essence of social dancing. Couples who communicate clearly – dance as one – are rare. When the partnership is powerful it is difficult to perceive one dancer without the other. The "look," the gentle caress, the respectful lead by the gentleman and the subsequent completion of the pattern by his lady honor the etiquette of the social contract.

> *Partner dancing is a conversation. Dancers (must) relate to each other through the music. (Cathi Nyemchek, U.S. 10-Dance Champion)*

THE SOCIAL CONTRACT
In Business And In Life

The relationship between the work that needs to be done and the people who need to do it will always be a key business issue. Despite claims to the contrary, businesses are forcing people to measure success by "the numbers." The tendency to squeeze success into analytical abstractions distorts and oversimplifies the richness of work. It insists on evaluating performance through ratings and lists, matrices and 360 surveys to guarantee proverbial bottom lines. When businesses overlook the human side of quality, that collective esprit de corps that defies the economic calculus of motives of top management, it does so at its own peril.

Businesses that cannot or will not allow people to shed their "data clothes" would be wise to consider lifestyle contracts. If businesses continue to place profit and cost control ahead of employee loyalty and mutual respect they are neglecting the human side of quality and violating the lifestyle contract. The thin veil of decency often called the business code of conduct is all that separates most employees from the tyranny of excessive profit motives and human capital exploitation that lie dormant beneath most businesses' thickly-veneered human relations surface.

TIP FROM YOUR COACHES: Develop a Social Contract within your partnerships. Here's how: create a list of behaviors that have sabotaged previous partnerships and a list of behaviors that built and sustained positive partnerships. Have all stakeholders agree to eliminate the negatives and practice the positives. This seemingly simple task will be well worth the time you invest – we promise!

SPACESHIFTING

Lyrically, dancers have the freedom to shift energies and identities to musically interpret a particular dance. For example, the Foxtrot is a stylish, playful dance, so ballroom competitors or social dancers must shift their energy and dance persona to characterize the playfulness, smoothness and upbeat nature of the Foxtrot. Conversely, the rumba is a romantic, sensual dance which requires couples to assume romantic roles, tightly wrapped around the sensuality of the dance.

Spaceshifting is the rhythmic soul of the dance. The style, musicality, and lyrical nature of any dance demand energy changes and personality changes in the dancers. Spaceshifting requires couples to "step" into the archetypal character of the dance. It is transformative, emotionally freeing and allows couples to transcend the ordinary.

Spaceshifting is zeppelin-like – it lifts the spirit and fills the dancer's body with the soul of the dance. Couples move beyond the boundaries of individual personalities and shift into a higher, more transcendental self. Unconscious parts of dancers surface and couples discover there is more to partnership than me-ness as they uncover hidden synergistic talents. Eventually, it becomes easier to "step" in and out of dance characters as the couples progress.

The practiced "shifting" creates a more fluid and flexible unit, a more confident, shiftier one that is able to morph their own uniqueness into each dance. The capacity to be different "selves" is a necessary skill for competitive dancers. Those who pull it off become one with the music, adding liquid grace to every step, arm gesture and spin.

SPACE SHIFTING
In Business And In Life

People are invited to many "dances" during the course of a day: the total population meeting waltz; the virtual project quickstep; the performance review cha-cha; the client needs assessment tango; the family dinner mambo; the get-everyone-to-their-activities foxtrot, the weekend fun jive, and so on. Each "dance" requires a shift in the person's thinking, input and persona. People must shift their projected "self" depending on which space(i.e. meeting or one-on-one interaction) requires their presence.

Spaceshifting is not the same thing as facade. Facade is retailing pretense and deceit. Spaceshifting is professional savoir-faire, the ability to wear the particular organizational hat which suits the occasion. Spaceshifting requires people to "step into the archetypal character of the dance" to add the right amounts of tact, diplomacy, technical expertise, wise counsel, political clout, enthusiasm, humor, insight, judgment, information dumps, etc.

In a very real sense every business dance (social interaction) is a performance review, so an individual's professional choreography must shine. Spaceshifting is an excellent strategy to make a good impression. Those who pull it off become one with the music, adding liquid grace to every meeting, family gathering or social setting.

TIP FROM YOUR COACHES: Take time to assess the character of the relationships involved in each interaction. Determine the mood of the "dance", and make a conscious decision about how you want to present yourself in the situation. By applying the Space Shifting concept, you will be able to project the best "you" that you can be!

STACCATO

The Paso Doble and Flamenco are staccatoed dances. They are hot, macho and impassioned. Limbs flicker like flames bursting from erect, Flamenco-styled bodies. The dancer's soul is ablaze, illuminating every heel snap and head jerk. The dancers articulate the drama between man, cape and sacrificial bull. Feet appear to dance on the sands of a bull fighting arena. Hands gesture majestically and dramatize righteous fury. Head snaps and steeled eyes focus on metaphorical bulls.

In staccato the dancers are on fire. Yin and Yang energies are awakened. Body heat and wired emotions fuel the dance with unbounded fervor. Lines erupt out of curves, sending the dancers into leaps, turns and stalks. In the Paso Doble the man is the matador and the woman his imaginary cape. Feelings are as staccatoed as the music. Exhilaration, triumph, courage, determination, defiance, calculatedness, contempt are the parade of emotions which carry the dance.

The Paso Doble and Flamenco are powerful dances. They are conquests of cunning, restlessness, and obsession. They are mercurial in nature, masterpieces of raw, unbridled energy which transfuse spirit into matter. They represent the part of us that wants to be free, unbridled, untethered, wild and adventurous. They are the rebellious us, the prince-of-tides part of us. They represent the Olympian us, the us that cannot be boxed, packaged, sold, or controlled. They're the invincible us, the impregnable us, the Zen us.

> Dance is one of the most powerful forms of magical ritual...it is an outer expression of the inner spirit.
> (Ted Andrews)

STACCATO
In Business And In Life

Lifestyle staccato is defiance, contempt and impatience with any barrier that interferes with life, liberty and the pursuit of happiness. The obstacles can be interpersonal, operational or structural, but whatever their source, they cause people to boil at different degrees. Sometimes they cause people to go ballistic. Other times people form posses to track down happiness "thieves."

Lifestyle staccato generally occurs when people have a high sense of mission, uncommon sense, incredible synergy and an unfailing desire to achieve something important. Obstacles are seen as bandits, things which could steal happiness and rob us of our joy. Quarrels with obstacles make "staccatoed" people intolerant of anything which comes close to suffocating freedom and independence.

The challenge for "staccatoed" people is to control their impatience with lethargic bureaucrats, consensus worshippers, and pushy people. The good news is that people turbo-charged with Paso instincts and Flamenco proclivities can also be connoisseurs of cool. That's what makes them such good problem-solvers and barrier bashers. When difficulties arise, their "souls are ablaze...and wired emotions...send them into leaps, turns and stalks" to vanquish any and all lifestyle thieves.

TIP FROM YOUR COACHES: Face your obstacles with lifestyle staccato. Express your frustration and impatience in positive ways as you challenge the status quo. Remember the quote by Duke Ellington: *"I simply used the energy it takes to pout and wrote the blues."* That's lifestyle staccato!

SYNC OR SINK

The site of the annual Blackpool Dance Festival is in the carnival atmosphere of a seaside resort called Blackpool, England. The principle reason Blackpool is the Mecca for ballroom enthusiasts worldwide is the majestic Winter Garden Ballroom. Blackpool is the Super Bowl, the World Cup, the Cannes Film Festival of International ballroom dancing. Blackpool determines the world champions of Standard and Latin dances. Seventy-eight years of hosting championships has made Blackpool the most prestigious and the most resistant to change international dance community in the world of ballroom dancing.

Media passes for photographers, writers, editors and videographers are discouraged. Only a few official photographers are permitted to take pictures at approved festival locations. Television cameras are permitted solely to cover selected events on videotape. No film coverage of any kind is released to the networks.

As the sport moves toward wider coverage elsewhere, Blackpool founders and organizers of the most celebrated ballroom dance event in the history of dance will probably have get in sync with the times, or sink, and risk becoming history. Every profession has its own peculiar rhythms, rigors, hazards and joys. The business of ballroom dancing is no exception. The issue is the collision between colonial tradition and millennium realities. What do you hold on to? What do you release? To what extent do you value tradition over novelty? These are the questions Blackpool organizers must ask in the media-driven, sound-byte obsessed new millennium.

SYNC OR SINK
In Business And In Life

There is nothing more frustrating or debilitating than a team filled with members having different visions of success. When team members are out of sync with the mission of the team, it is a sure thing that they will sink in their efforts to succeed. The same is true of any partnership.

Success in life requires a constant willingness to revisit your mission, values, goals and procedures. Being in sync means that everyone involved is on the same page. But you must be sure the page you are on is current! Too many companies go down the proverbial tubes because they are focused on their current *product*, but forget what *business* they are in. Change is inevitable, and to be successful in life, you must be willing and able to adapt to the changes you face. But you must also be in sync with your own personal values and beliefs.

Unfortunately, businesses obsessed with technology and frightened by competitive obsolescence are more likely to de-value their human resources. When this happens, they find themselves constantly be out-of-sync with the manic gyrations of a schizophrenic business. People faced with these challenges will have to ask themselves whether they want to stay in sync with an organization's attempt to manage change, sink with the mediocrity of an uncaring business, or get in sync with a lifestyle that says: "If you're not finding joy in your work, you're paying too high a price."

TIP FROM YOUR COACHES: Revisit the goals of your team to be sure they are in sync with the current business realities. Also check your personal satisfaction meter to be sure your work is in sync with your values and beliefs. If you're out of sync, you're going to sink!

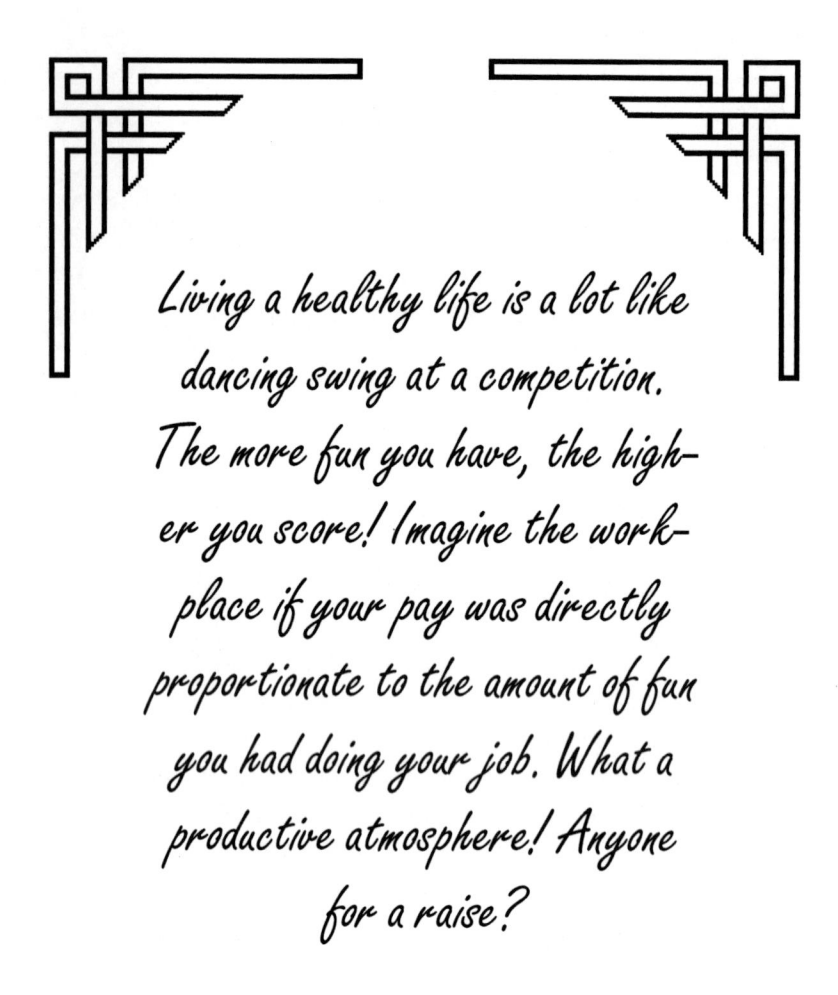

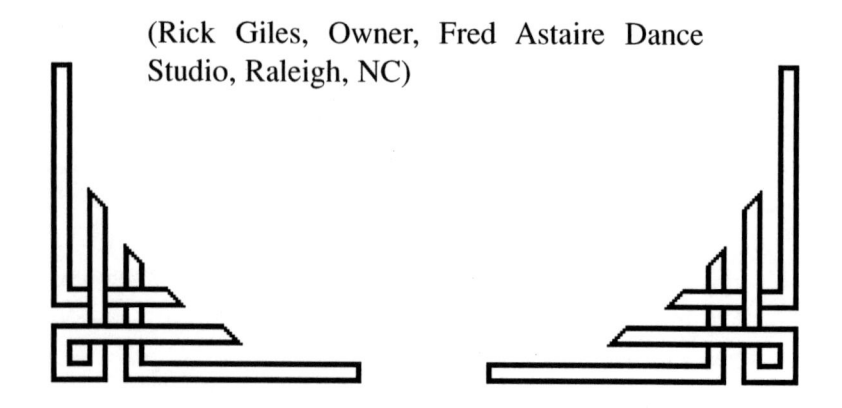

Living a healthy life is a lot like dancing swing at a competition. The more fun you have, the higher you score! Imagine the workplace if your pay was directly proportionate to the amount of fun you had doing your job. What a productive atmosphere! Anyone for a raise?

(Rick Giles, Owner, Fred Astaire Dance Studio, Raleigh, NC)

DANCE WISDOM
(Ask yourself: How do these quotes relate to my business and my life?)

It's the passion to dance that makes dancers, not the right physical type.
(Daniel Nagrin, legendary dancer, Professor Emeritus, Arizona State University)

Good partnerships and dancing have a lot in common: neither is learned by reading a book. You have to get out on the dance floor and experience it!
(Cher Holton)

Athletic trainers are usually in daily contact with the athletes they train: many sports medicine physicians have participated in the sports of the athletes they treat; sports scientists know the techniques involved in the sports they analyze. In contrast, most physicians have relatively little access to the daily interplay between dancers and their (craft)...We contend that the more physicians learn about the training, (competition) and activity of dancers prior to and at the time of injury, the better able they will be to manage... dance injuries.
(Ruth Soloman, director of dance-theater arts University of California)

The dance of God goes on without hands and feet.
(Kabir)

THE SYNTAX OF PERFORMANCE

The word syntax is defined as "the way words are put together to form phrases and sentences." Similarly, ballroom dancing at its best consists of elegantly choreographed movements linked to school figures and tested by floorcraft in a setting which demands excellence in styled movements, technical virtuosity, heart, energy and stamina.

The syntax of performance is the "spine" of the dance and there is always a subtext: controlled movements. To be in control is to be constantly recovering from losing control. All ballroom dancers know this! Every craft, art and employment has a unique "spine" which defines it and ensures its integrity. Physical appearance while dancing is the dancer's spine.

What appears on the surface as effortlessness and controlled has its invisible partners of inner contradiction and abandon. There must be a focus and accounting for every action, no matter how minute. The syntax of performance must be correct and definable at all times both internally and externally. Thousands of hours of repetitive practice sculpt the couple's unique style as a visual medium. The off-spring of repetition—flawless performance—is what makes the couple's choreography memorable.

The best dancers do not give their audiences forgeries. Their syntax is perfect. The goal is to achieve technical excellence while using the dance routine as a metaphor for exemplary teamwork, given the confines of the crowded dance floor and the mood of the dance. That is what makes the dance performance valid in the eyes of the judges and adoring audiences.

THE SYNTAX OF PERFORMANCE
In Business And In Life

The scarecrow power of uncertainty has little effect on people with highly developed lifestyle syntax. Lifestyle syntax is character forged in the crucible of living life in the trenches. You can tell what a person's ideals are by what he/she advocates, allows to go unchallenged and tolerates on a regular basis. Highly "syntaxed" people value principle, integrity and ethics above policies, procedures and rules and the proverbial bottom line. They know that a person's fate depends on strength of character, regardless of what life may dish out.

Highly successful people strengthen their lifestyle syntax because they know that character is a talisman. It is the anchor of personal conduct, the "spine" of both their personal and professional lives which allows authentic people to stand ramrod straight in the face of towering obstacles.

Successful partnerships emerge when the individuals involved in that partnership both possess highly developed lifestyle syntax. When they both come from a foundation of values, ethics and positive attitudes, they can face their "performance" knowing they are strong, prepared and ready to face any challenge.

TIP FROM YOUR COACHES: You are always setting an example by your behavior, your decisions, your words. Is your example one that others should follow?

TWINKLE

A step in any direction followed by a close, or near closing of the feet to establish a change of direction is called a twinkle. Twinkles are transition steps requiring a toe step to exit from the twinkle. They link dance steps and patterns to smooth movements, creating a graceful flow to changes in the dance progression. Complete twinkles consist of two full measures of rhythmical beats to keep dancers on beat for the next series of moves. There are many varieties of twinkles, including: single, triple, promenade, continuity, zigzag, spot and progressive.

Professional dancers know how to use the twinkle to move around the ballroom floor successfully. Whenever the pair meets an obstacle, such as another couple suddenly spinning into their path, they can execute a twinkle to change direction. They do it without missing a beat, with smiles hiding the irritation at having their well-choreographed move sabotaged. For all the audience knows, that twinkle was supposed to happen.

The twinkle also helps the couple transition from one choreographed figure to the next, and to navigate around the corners of the ballroom. While it seems like a rather insignificant step, the twinkle is actually one of the cornerstones of professional dancing. Couples practice this figure until they can perform it with perfection, on demand. Their skill in this transitional figure is often what separates the top couples from the rest of the pack.

> *The good life is a process, not a state of being. It is a direction, not a destination. (Carl Rogers)*

TWINKLE
In Business And In Life

Events in life often hit you out of the blue, and interfere with all your well-choreographed plans. Your ability to twinkle – transition around obstacles and change direction with ease and grace – will help make life more bearable – and more fun.

What are the twinkles in business and in life? They include the ability to stay focused; to look for solutions rather than place blame; to practice proven stress-busters; to maintain a healthy body; to strengthen our spiritual base and keep it active; to be able to forgive, release and move on; to appreciate the simple joys of life; to value and respect others.

The list could go on and on. The point is that you will never make it around the ballroom of life without obstacles and corners to navigate. When the problems and frustrations occur, it's too late to start practicing your twinkles. They must be firmly entrenched in your mind, body and soul. At the drop of a hat, you must be able to execute the twinkle, with a smile. For all anyone knows, the twinkle was planned in your choreography.

TIP FROM YOUR COACHES: Build a repertoire of stress-busters and practice using them when you are not under any particular stress. These strategies and techniques become your "basic twinkle", helping you successfully navigate life's obstacles, barriers, and surprises.

VERBAL SPLINTERS

Research shows that verbal attacks by a student's overly-critical teacher/coach lower the dancer's self esteem and self-confidence. Dancers who experience excessive amounts of toxic criticism suffer from chronic fear, doubt, and physical exertion. Self-sabotage, driven by consistent doubt, leads to paranoia, poor dance performance, performance anxiety and injury. These "verbal splinters" become emotional stakes-in-the-heart as students react to unwarranted censure.

Personal attacks launched by teachers or coaches generally come from people who are stuck on themselves and their reputations. Hurtful criticism is a tell-tale sign of an authority figure who has lost his/her edge. The best teachers, coaches and choreographers know that any teaching role is a gate-keeping role. It is meant to open doors, not shove students through them.

In the dance business, students and competitors alike know that cruel teachers and coaches describe themselves as paragons of frankness to hide their brutality. Only a few of the most political or hopelessly needy performers allow themselves to fall victim to a continual barrage of "verbal splinters." Other, more confident and self-assured students use dignified "tweezers" to permanently extract bothersome splinters and move on to a coach who knows how to give sane feedback.

> *As we recognize that all conflict gives us an opportunity to dance rather than struggle, our movements and actions take on a spirit of joy and harmony that permeates all concerned. (Thomas Crum)*

VERBAL SPLINTERS
In Business And In Life

The toughest type of feedback people have to give and receive is constructive criticism. In fact, one of our favorite quotes is: "Constructive criticism is difficult to take – especially from friends, family members, coworkers, superiors, and strangers." Verbal splinters in business and in life are ill-considered attempts to provide feedback that results in hurtful criticism being leveled at someone. Whether these toxic salvos are intentional or irresponsible doesn't matter, "barbs and splinters" hurt and the outcome is a wounded relationship.

Highly successful people keep work areas and family settings as "splinter-free" as possible by following a few feedback principles. They keep criticism *private*, recognizing that no one appreciates public humiliation. They keep feedback *positively-framed* and f*ocused on the objectionable behavior* instead of attacking someone's self-esteem. Feedback is kept *specific and descriptive* so remedial actions are doable and measurable.

Examples of how to do something better are provided so the negligent colleague, relative or friend knows what success looks like. *Positive reinforcement is provided* once the person demonstrates his/her newly acquired skills. Feedback offered in this fashion turns "lifestyle splinters" into magic wands of social grace.

TIP FROM YOUR COACHES: Use the Splinter-Free Principles listed above to critique the feedback you provide to others. It is an excellent idea to practice the feedback (out loud) before actually confronting the individual.

VOLTÃ

The voltã is a samba move which is so full of rhythm and pizzazz it has become a classic figure in dance. In the voltã, the gentleman's and lady's paths cross over each other in what can be described as a curved X movement as they progress along the dance floor. It extends the "slow-a-slow" rhythm across two bars of music and is generally counted as 1-a-2-a-3-a-4-a. The couple first dances parallel, then the gentleman lifts the lady's hand so she can pass under his arm and in front of him as they form an intersection. Once the couple dismounts from the voltã, they simply dance into the next figure or movement.

In the voltã, two opposing energies (the man and the woman) are on the same trajectory and pass each other without colliding to produce a stylish and energetic outcome. Travelling voltãs allow each dancer to "see the world" from the partner's position. The juxtaposition of the dancers requires an exactness that belies the serendipitous nature of the playful encounter. The near collision which characterizes the calculus of movements (syzygy) made by the pair is more illusionary than real as the partners seem to occupy the same space at the same time.

We ought to dance with rapture that we should be alive, and in the flesh, and part of the living, incarnate cosmos. (D. H. Lawrence)

VOLTÃ
In Business And In Life

Our ability to understand someone else's point of view is called empathy. It is the act of "walking a mile in another person's shoes." When an entire team or family adopts this empathetic response, it is called lifestyle voltã. It stems from an awareness that there is a human side to business and family relationships that transcends individual goals, schedules and interests. Lifestyle voltã is a way for people to avoid becoming fragmented or separated by differing viewpoints, values or directions.

For example, when the going gets tough and you find yourself headed toward a cul-de-sac of melancholy, the call must be for a lifestyle voltã. The emphasis on feelings allows the silent wailing or loud displeasure of an apprehensive teammate, relative or friend to be addressed.

The cathartic effects of lifestyle voltã can galvanize a team and solidify a family. Openly sharing points of view without fear of reprisal is a powerful forum for self-disclosure. Making time in busy schedules to pass each other without colliding is critical. Being able to "get into each other's heads" and see something from their point of view is crucial. Once people feel mutual respect for another's share of the load, interpersonal collisions become lifestyle voltãs allowing us to use empathy as a buffer to unite us.

TIP FROM YOUR COACHES: Use lifestyle voltã to see the world from your partner's point of view. Build in time, no matter how busy the schedule, to share a cup of coffee or tea and talk.

WALTZ

It is not an exaggeration to say that the slow Waltz is perhaps the favorite formal dance of all time. It is the dance of choice at weddings and most formal occasions, and is generally associated with an evening's last dance. It is used for celebrations, inaugurations and coronations. The slow waltz and its faster cousin, the Viennese Waltz are the only dances that link romance (respectable or forbidden) with adult life's happier moments. Each is a dance of romance, sophistication and gallantry. The Waltz brings a gentleman and his lady into a partnership of mutual admiration and respect as the couple sways, pivots and chassés across the floor.

Although both waltzes are Austrian folk dances called Ländberg, the dances have never lost their universal appeal as the most elegant, stately and ostentatious creations in ballroom pageantry. The slow, romantic rise and fall of the slow waltz symbolizes the sense of peace and serenity sought by everyone who wants to step out of the toils of every day life into a few cubic feet of joy and reverence. The speed and vigor of the majestic Viennese Waltz takes couples into a fantasyland of elegance, aristocracy and royalty as they rocket across the floor to show the world that they are oblivious to its rigors and disappointments.

Waltzing is life at its fullest, finest and best. Cares become caresses and disappointments become appointments with destiny.

> *The earth sets some music going in us and dance we must. (Edgar Lee Masters, Spoon River Anthology)*

WALTZ
In Business And In Life

It is not an exaggeration to say that lifestyle waltzes could be one of our favorite activities. Metaphorically speaking, lifestyle waltzes could be the activity of choice whenever we want to celebrate our success or share in someone else's. The celebration does not have to be elaborate, although it can be depending on your budget and interest. A lifestyle "waltz" is the acknowledgement of work's happier moments. It is a celebratory event that links recognition and reward with performance and achievement.

Whether you choose to throw an extravaganza (Viennese Waltz) or settle for a modest pat on the back, group cheer or thank you notes (slow waltzes), the atmosphere should be festive enough to celebrate an important accomplishment. The value of a well-orchestrated lifestyle waltz is that it helps you appreciate your collective achievements.

So often we focus on what we've done wrong. We burden each other with regrets, disappointments and ought-to-haves. When you fail to routinely celebrate accomplishments, you are crawling instead of waltzing through life.

TIP FROM YOUR COACHES: Use lifestyle waltzes as moments of celebration and recognition. When you feel the spirit strike, simply turn to your teammates, family members or partners and say with a bow or curtsy, "Shall we dance?" Then, let the waltz begin!

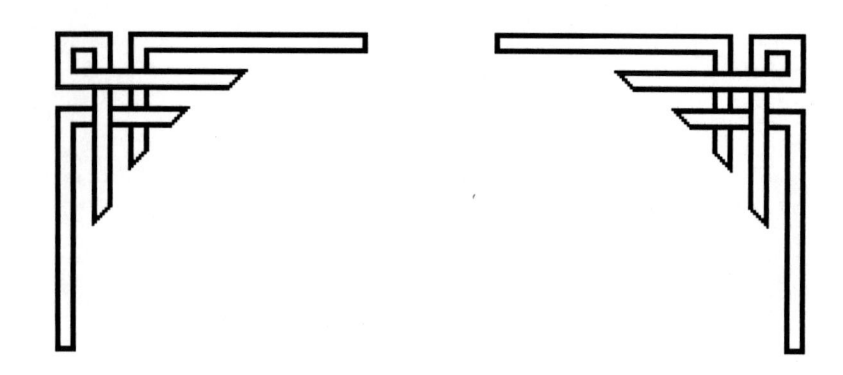

A coach is like a parent, guiding and sharing the experiences of life and teaching the qualities of dance.

(Sam Sodano, Chairman of the Arthur Murray International Dance Board)

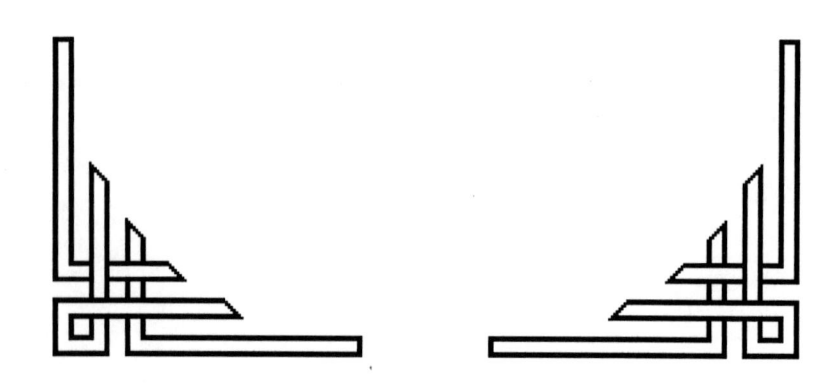

DANCE WISDOM
(Ask yourself: How do these quotes relate to my business and my life?)

I encourage (dancers) to study from as many different teachers as possible, even if it means going to other studios. When you work in a variety of styles, you're able to adjust to...different choreography. If you can only dance one style, you're limited.
(Tina Landon, choreographer– Janet Jackson's World Tours)

Dancers who try to overly stand out...really bother me. All they need to do is the work. When they're too much in my face, or overly dressed, or have too much make-up on, or too much hair, I...pull away. I can't see the (real dancer) for all the stuff.
(Otis Sallid, choreographer of the 1997 Academy Awards)

If it's the last dance, dance backwards.
(Bo)

What could be more exhilarating than dancing on your own edge – leaping into the dark fueled purely by faith in your own potential to become living art?
(Gaberielle Roth, theater director, dance teacher, recording artist)

ABOUT THE AUTHORS

Bil and Cher Holton are a dynamic team: they are dance partners, business partners and marriage partners! When they work with clients to build strong team relationships, they come from a solid foundation of personal experience.

Since 1984 they have worked with clients worldwide through their firm, The Holton Consulting Group, Inc., focusing on "The Human Side of Quality." Their impressive client list includes Fortune 500 companies, government agencies, healthcare organizations, small businesses and educational institutions.

In addition to their popular TurboTeam Development™ and TurboTraining™ consulting responsibilities, both Bil and Cher are keynote speakers. Cher focuses on "Living at the Speed of Life: Staying in Control in a World Gone Bonkers, while Bil portrays John Doe, ordinary citizen, patriotic American, Ambassador for the American Dream and the Power of Responsible Choice.

Bil and Cher are also Amateur Couple Ballroom Dancers. They have won national student-level championships in waltz, foxtrot, tango, viennesse waltz, rumba, east coast swing and cha-cha. They have also taken awards for their Theatre Arts and Solo Couple routines.

MORE BOOKS BY THE HOLTONS

America Is My Home: the Story of Uncle Sam: the Myth, the Man and the Acronym (Bil Holton, 2001)

Suppose: Questions to Turbo-Charge Team Culture (Bil Holton and Cher Holton2000)

The Manager's Short Course (1992); Second edition– *The Manager's Short Course to a Long Career* (Bil Holton and Cher Holton, 1999)

Living at the Speed of Light: Staying in Control in a World Gone Bonkers! (Cher Holton, 1999)

From Battlefield to Boardroom: Leadership Lessons of Robert E. Lee (Bil Holton, 1995; 1998)

From Battlefield to Bottomline: Leadership Lessons of Ulysses S. Grant (Bil Holton, 1995; 1999)

Business Prayers for Millennium Managers (Bil Holton and Cher Holton, currently in press).

Right-Sizing America: 21st Century Wisdom for Millennium Americans (Bil Holton, currently in press).

HOW TO CONTACT THE HOLTONS

We invite you to grab a cup of coffee, tea or a soda and visit us at www.holtonconsulting.com.